Joseph,
A Passage to God's Covenant

Biblical figures 3

Joseph,
A Passage to God's Covenant

Dr. Jaerock Lee

URIM
BOOKS

Joseph, A Passage to God's Covenant by Dr. Jaerock Lee
Published by Urim Books (Representative: Johnny H.Kim)
73, Yeouidaebang-ro 22-gil, Dongjak-gu, Seoul, Korea
www.urimbooks.com

All rights reserved. This book or parts thereof may not be reproduced in any form, stored in a retrieval system, or transmitted in any form or by any means, electronic, mechanical, photocopying, recording or otherwise, without prior written permission of the publisher.

Unless otherwise noted, all Scripture quotations are taken from the Holy Bible, NEW AMERICAN STANDARD BIBLE, ®, Copyright © 1960, 1962, 1963, 1968, 1971, 1972, 1973, 1975, 1977, 1995 by The Lockman Foundation. Used by permission.

Copyright © 2018 by Dr. Jaerock Lee
ISBN: 979-11-263-1367-9 03230
Translation Copyright © 2017 by Dr. Esther K. Chung. Used by permission.

Previously published in Korean by Urim Books in Seoul, Korea in 2015

First Edition: July 2024

Edited by Dr. Geumsun Vin
Designed by Design Team of Urim Books
For more information contact: urimbook@hotmail.com

"God sent me before you
to preserve for you a remnant in the earth,
and to keep you alive
by a great deliverance.
Now, therefore, it was not you
who sent me here, but God;
and He has made me a father to Pharaoh
and lord of all his household
and ruler over all the land of Egypt."

(Genesis 45:7-8)

· Foreword ·

Joseph, a Dreamer and a Passageway of God's Covenant

About 4,000 years ago, there was a person who rose up to the position of the prime minister from the bottom of the social ladder. He is Joseph, who saved numerous lives from the great famine that lasted seven years in the Near East. He also laid the foundation for the nation of Israel, which serves as a case-example in human cultivation.

Abraham, the father of faith begot Isaac, and Abraham's son Isaac begot Jacob. Jacob begot twelve sons from four wives, and Joseph is the eleventh.

Genesis 37:2 says, *"These are the records of the generations of Jacob."* The passage talks about the behaviors of the 17-year-old Joseph, the reactions of his brothers, and his two unusual dreams.

The contents of the dreams are as follows: for the first dream, Joseph was binding the sheaves on the field, and the sheaves bound by his brothers bowed down to the sheaf bound by Joseph. The second one was that the sun and the moon and eleven stars bowed down to Joseph. These dreams were given by God. It meant Joseph would become a noble person and his parents and brothers would honor him.

Why would the contents of Joseph's dream be written in the generations of Jacob? It's because Joseph's life itself serves as the process and passageway for God's covenant that He made with Abraham, Isaac, and Jacob.

"He has remembered His covenant forever, the word which He commanded to a thousand generations, the covenant which He made with Abraham, and His oath to Isaac. Then He confirmed it to Jacob for a statute, to Israel as an everlasting covenant" (Psalm 105:8-11).

"And He called for a famine upon the land; He broke the whole staff of bread. He sent a man before them, Joseph, who was sold as a slave. They afflicted his feet with fetters, he himself was laid in irons; until the time that his word came to pass, the word of the LORD tested him" (Psalm 105:16-19).

Joseph was sold as a slave by his brothers. He was also imprisoned. It looks like his life was a failure. But these events were allowed by God in His plan and providence to establish Joseph as the prime minister of Egypt and to lay the foundation for the nation of Israel.

Joseph was never disheartened because he had the dream and vision given by God. He followed the way of righteousness by living a faithful and honest life. God made him prosperous wherever he went. God let him be loved and acknowledged by the people around him. Eventually, Joseph became the prime minister of Egypt by the guidance of God.

When the time came, his brothers bowed before Joseph. Of course, as for them they bowed before the prime minister of Egypt to get some food, but it was the fulfillment of the God-given dream.

Joseph didn't harbor any resentment or hard-feelings toward his brothers for having sold him as a slave. He only showed wisdom of goodness so that his brothers could demolish the wall of sin standing between them and God through true repentance and they could become the foundations of the twelve tribes of Israel. Joseph showed a very deep level of love to save everyone, going beyond just the level of forgiveness.

The reason why God created human beings on this earth and has cultivated them for such a long time is to get true children with whom

He can share love forever. God chose a nation to be the example for all other nations in the course of human cultivation. God first chose Abraham as the father of faith, and He laid the foundation of the nation of Israel through the twelve sons of Jacob.

In this process, Joseph led his entire family to Egypt. This way, the family could be protected from the threats of other neighboring peoples, and Israel could become a big people within the short period of 430 years.

In Egypt it seemed Joseph's life was being lowered for a moment, but it was in fact a trial of blessing and the shortcut to blessing. It's because Joseph believed the good will of God would be fulfilled; he depended on God alone, believing that his dream given by God would be fulfilled.

I hope all the readers of this book will meet the God of blessing who was with Joseph and learn the secrets to prosperous life. I hope they will also learn good principles of leadership from Joseph's example and become the passageways to fulfill the providence of God at the end time.

I give thanks to Geumsun Vin the director of the Editorial Bureau of Manmin Central Church and the staff of Urim Books who made this publication possible. I give all thanks and glory to God the Father who has guided us.

· Prologue 1 ·

Family tree of Joseph, Prime Minister of Egypt

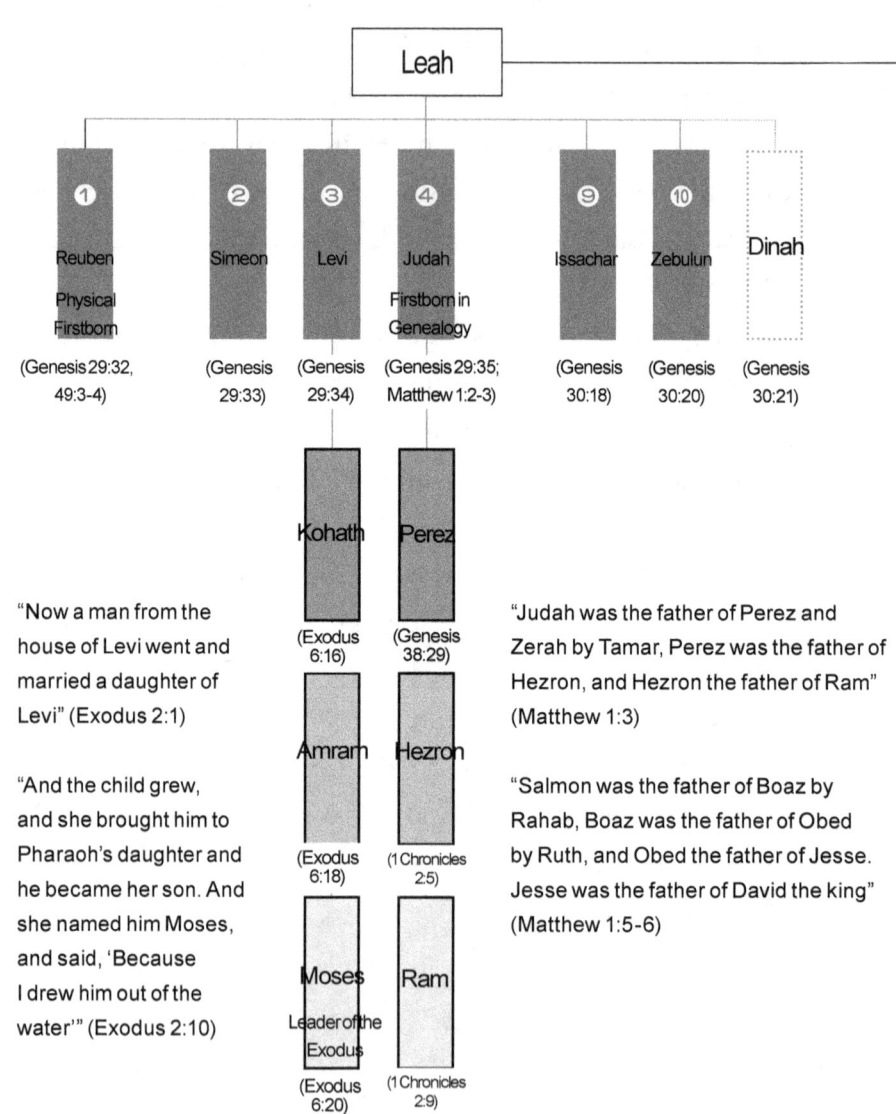

"Now a man from the house of Levi went and married a daughter of Levi" (Exodus 2:1)

"And the child grew, and she brought him to Pharaoh's daughter and he became her son. And she named him Moses, and said, 'Because I drew him out of the water'" (Exodus 2:10)

"Judah was the father of Perez and Zerah by Tamar, Perez was the father of Hezron, and Hezron the father of Ram" (Matthew 1:3)

"Salmon was the father of Boaz by Rahab, Boaz was the father of Obed by Ruth, and Obed the father of Jesse. Jesse was the father of David the king" (Matthew 1:5-6)

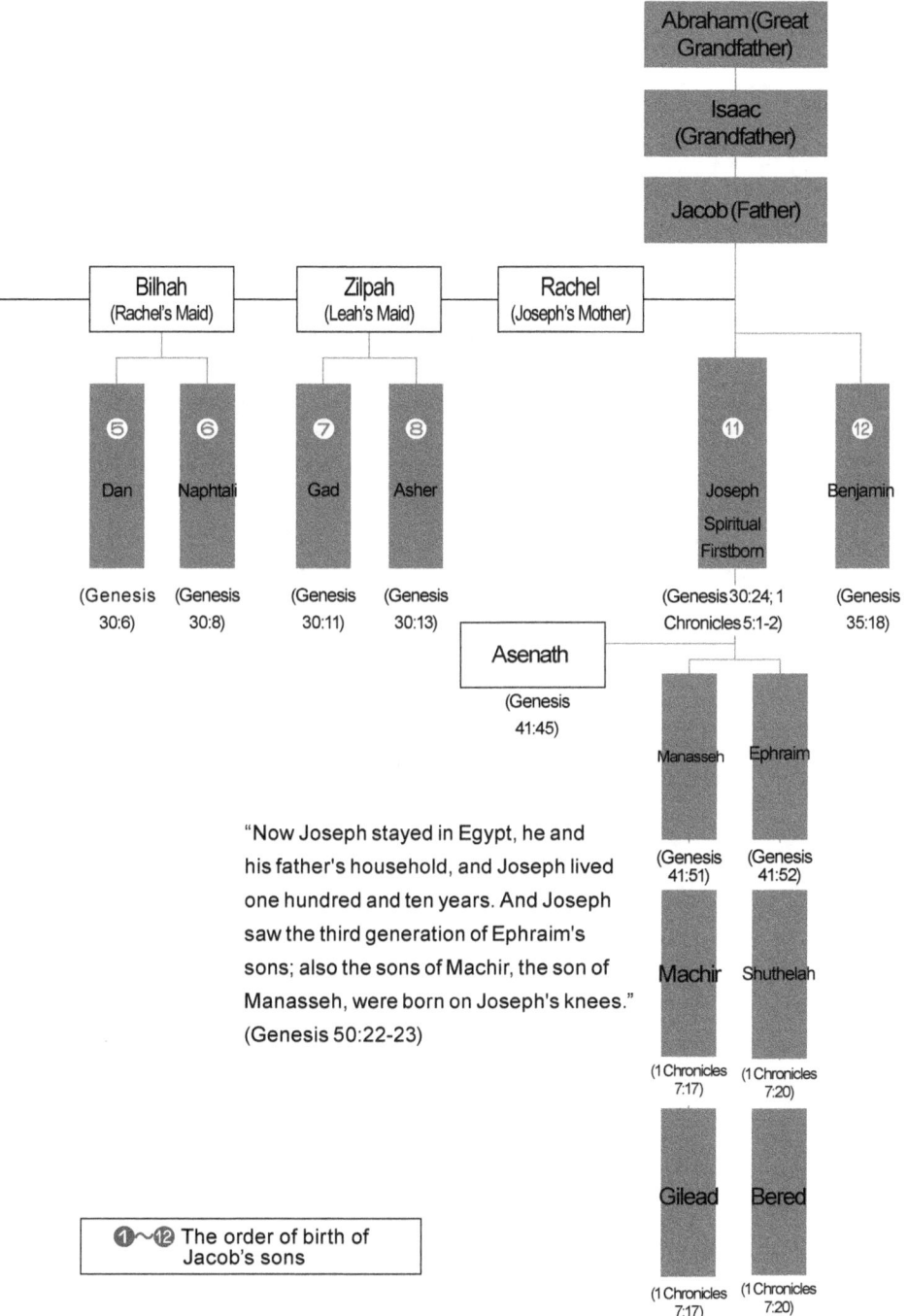

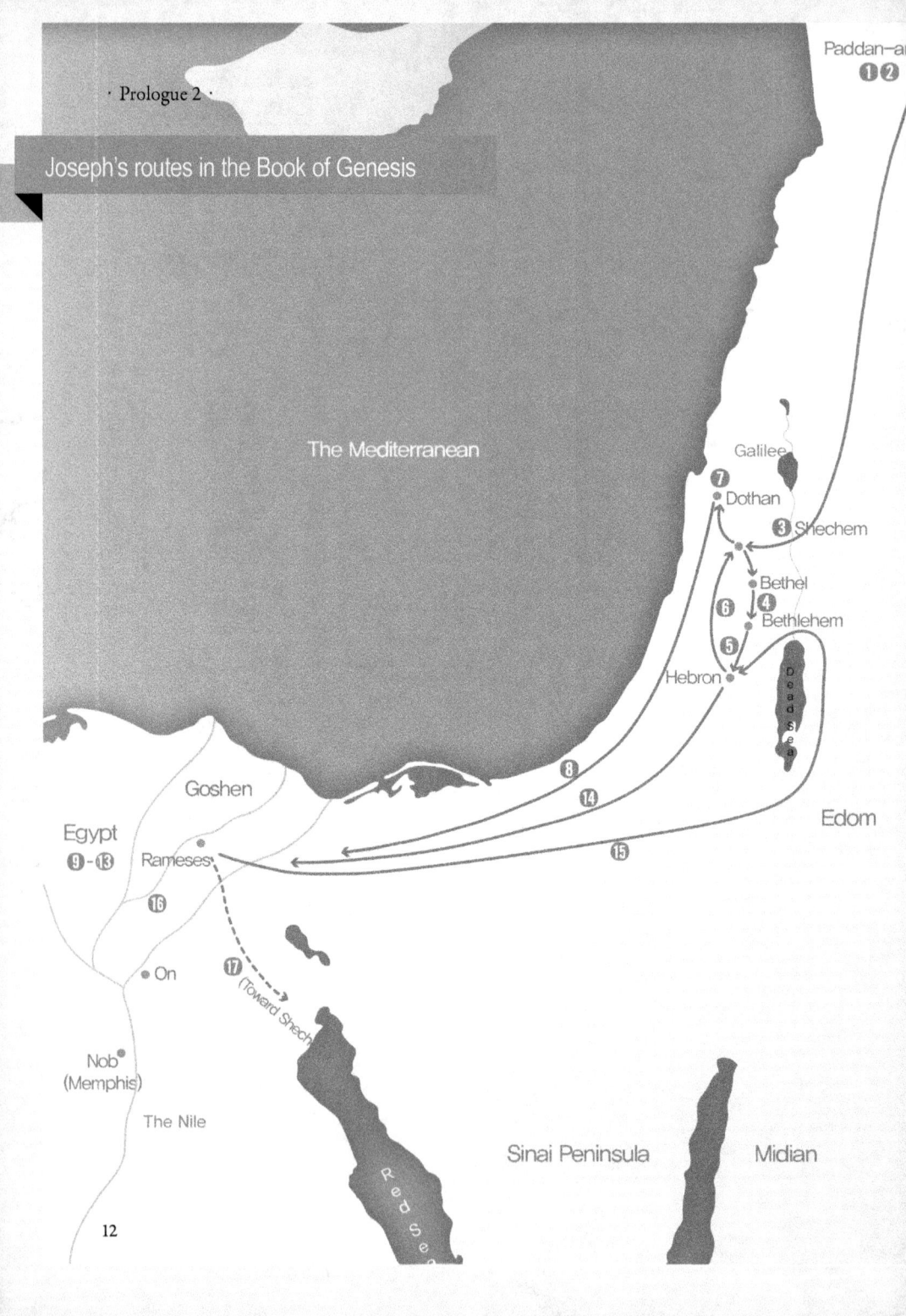

⟨From birth to age 17⟩

❶ Joseph was born as the eleventh son of Jacob at Paddan-aram (Genesis 30:24)
❷ After his birth, his father Jacob made an agreement with Laban and became very rich (Genesis 30:25-31)
❸ Joseph's family crossed Jabbok River and settled down in Shechem (Genesis 33)
❹ After the incident involving Dinah, they left Shechem and set out for Hebron. Joseph's mother Rachel died while giving birth to Benjamin and was buried on the way to Bethlehem (Genesis 35:19)
❺ He reached Hebron with his father Jacob and met his grandfather Isaac (Genesis 35:27)
❻ He went to Shechem looking for his brothers by the request of his father (Genesis 37:14)
❼ He reached Dothan with the help of an angel and met his brothers (Genesis 37:17)
❽ He was sold as a slave into Egypt by the hands of his brothers (Genesis 37:28)

⟨From age 17 to age 30⟩

❾ He was sold to Potiphar, the captain of the bodyguard of Egypt, and became general manager of his household (Genesis 39:4)
❿ He was wrongfully accused and was put into the jail for prisoners of the king (Genesis 39:20)
⓫ He interpreted the king's dream and became the prime minister 13 years after he went to Egypt (Genesis 41)

⟨From age 30 to age 110⟩

⓬ He inspected the whole land of Egypt and made provisions for the 7-year famine as the prime minister (Genesis 41:46-48)
⓭ He met his brothers in the second year of the famine and helped them change with good wisdom (Genesis 42-45)
⓮ He led Jacob and his family to settle down in Goshen, Egypt (Genesis 46-49)
⓯ He had a grand funeral for his father and buried him in Hebron in the land of Canaan (Genesis 50:7-13)
⓰ He died in Egypt at the age of 110 (Genesis 50)
⓱ According to his will, Moses brought up Joseph's remains (Genesis 50:25; Exodus 13:19)

Contents

Foreword
Prologue   1. Family tree of Joseph, Prime Minister of Egypt · 10
           2. Joseph's routes in the Book of Genesis · 12

Part 1
A Hebrew Man, Joseph, Becomes Prime Minister of Egypt

Chapter 1   "How then could I do this great evil and sin against God?" · 23

   1. Joseph Is Sold into Potiphar's House
   2. Being in Charge of Whole Household of Potiphar
   3. Refusing the Seduction of Potiphar's Wife
   4. Wrongfully Accused by Potiphar's Wife
   5. Imprisoned in God's Providence
   # Add-in 1: The God of Abraham, the God Isaac, and the God of Jacob

Chapter 2   Interpreting the Dreams of the Cupbearer and the Baker · 47

   1. Joseph Serves the Two Officials in Jail
   2. Two Officials Get Concerned Over Their Dreams
   3. Joseph Interprets the Two Officials' Dreams
   4. Chief Cupbearer Forgets Joseph's Request
   # Add-in 2: What Kind of Country Was Ancient Egypt?

Chapter 3   The Hebrew Slave, Joseph, Becomes the Prime Minister · 61

    1. Pharaoh Has Strange Dreams
    2. The Chief Cupbearer Recommends Joseph
    3. Pharaoh Asks Joseph to Interpret His Dreams
    4. Joseph Suggests Detailed Provisions
    5. In Him is a Divine Spirit: "You Shall Be over My House"
    6. Prime Minister Joseph Prepares for Famine

Part 2

Joseph's Wisdom of Goodness Saves Israel and Egypt

Chapter 4   "Your Words May Be Tested, Whether There Is Truth in You" · 83

    1. Jacob's Ten Sons Went to Egypt to Buy Grain
    2. "Where Have You Come From? You Are Spies"
    3. Joseph Puts His Brothers in Prison
    4. "If You Are Honest Men, Bring Your Youngest Brother"
    5. Jacob Laments Saying He Will Also Lose Benjamin

Chapter 5   Return to Egypt with Benjamin · 99

    1. Judah Tries to Persuade Jacob
    2. Joseph's Brothers Took Benjamin to Egypt with Them
    3. Brothers Became Afraid When Brought to Joseph's House
    4. Joseph Sheds Tears of Thanksgiving
    5. Joseph Follows the Order and Duty of Men Precisely
    # Add-in 3: Levels of Forgiveness

Chapter 6   Joseph Changes His Brothers with Wisdom of Goodness · 119

    1. "Put My Silver Cup and His Money for the Grain in His Sack"
    2. Joseph Tests Love among His Brothers
    3. Judah Earnestly Pleas to Save Benjamin

Chapter 7   "You Must Hurry and Bring My Father Down Here" · 129

    1. "Do Not Be Grieved Because You Sold Me Here"
    2. "God Has Made Me Lord of All Egypt"
    3. "Take Your Father and Your Households and Come to Me"
    4. "I will Go and See Him before I Die"

Part 3

> Joseph, A Passageway to the Fulfillment of God's Covenant

Chapter 8 Jacob's Family in Goshen · 147

    1. "I Will Make You a Great Nation There"
    2. Jacob's Household Moved to Egypt
    3. When Pharaoh Calls You and Says, 'What is Your Occupation?'
    Add-in 4: The Promised Land of Canaan Given to Abraham, Isaac, and Jacob

Chapter 9 Joseph's Wisdom of Goodness and Policies for Famine · 161

    1. Joseph Considers All Details from Pharaoh's Perspective
    2. Getting Rameses through Joseph's Wisdom
    3. Joseph Deals with the Deepening Famine
    4. New Land Policy of Egypt
    5. Vowing to Bury Jacob in His Fathers' Burial Place

Chapter 10 Joseph's Sons, Manasseh and Ephraim · 177

    1. Joseph Sees Jacob at His Deathbed
    2. Jacob Blesses Joseph's Sons
    3. Jacob Puts Ephraim before Manasseh
    4. Jacob Gives More Inheritance to Joseph

Chapter 11 Jacob's Death and Last Will · 193

1. Jacob Summons His Sons before His Death
2. Reuben Loses His Birthright
3. Simeon and Levi Receive Retribution for their Wickedness
4. Prophecy of the Coming of the Messiah through Judah
5. Jacob's Last Will for Zebulun, Issachar, and Dan
6. Jacob's Last Will for Gad, Asher, and Naphtali
7. Jacob's Last Will for Joseph and Benjamin
8. Jacob's Request for His Burial in Canaan
Add-in 5: Israel Became a Big People in Egypt

Chapter 12 Jacob's Funeral and Joseph's Death · 215

1. Joseph Prepares Jacob's Funeral
2. "Let Me Go Up and Bury My Father"
3. Grand Funeral That Revealed God's Glory
4. "Do Not Be Afraid, For Am I In God's Place?"
5. "You Shall Carry My Bones Up from Here"
Add-in 6: Funerals of Egyptians and Hebrews

Epilogue
1. Joseph, the Passageway of God's Covenant · 234
2. Flaming Torch Covenant and Fulfillment of the Prophecy · 236
3. Promise about Canaan Land and Fulfillment · 240

"Father, my Father!
You fill my shortcomings and change me.
You give me the best things that You have.
How faithful my Father is!

I was immature but You changed me and gave me wisdom.
You let me overcome each moment in my life.
You let me know when to be silent and when to speak up.
You let me see the hearts of men and gain their hearts.
Father, my Father,
You let my cup overflow with Your blessings.

My Father,
You let me see the glory of this day,
By always comforting and strengthening me
to endure all things!

Part 1

A Hebrew Man, Joseph, Becomes Prime Minister of Egypt

Part 1

Through trials, we can become a proper instrument of God.
Trials are delicate hands of God.

Trials allowed to broaden our hearts are not caused by sins or evil, and thus God always accompanies us and intervenes in our lives.

A 30-year-old Hebrew man became the prime minister who ruled all over Egypt because he went through the trials very well.

Joseph
Chapter 1

"How then could I do this great evil and sin against God?"

Joseph Is Sold into Potiphar's House

Being in Charge of Whole Household of Potiphar

Refusing the Seduction of Potiphar's Wife

Wrongfully Accused by Potiphar's Wife

Imprisoned in God's Providence

1. Joseph Is Sold into Potiphar's House

Now Joseph had been taken down to Egypt; and Potiphar, an Egyptian officer of Pharaoh, the captain of the bodyguard, bought him from the Ishmaelites, who had taken him down there. The LORD was with Joseph, so he became a successful man. And he was in the house of his master, the Egyptian. Now his master saw that the LORD was with him and how the LORD caused all that he did to prosper in his hand. (39:1-3)

Jacob, the father of the people of Israel, had twelve sons whom he begot from four wives. Jacob favored Joseph whom he begot at a later stage of his life. He put a varicolored tunic on him. He always put him close and taught him the words of God. It's because Joseph was the son born of Rachel, Jacob's most favored wife, and he was obedient, good-hearted, and clever since childhood.

Joseph's brothers were jealous of him because their father loved Joseph more than them. To make things worse, Joseph also behaved in a way to make his brothers hate him. He made reports to his father of his brothers' faults (Genesis 37:2). However, he did not bring the reports with an evil intention; he wanted his father to know about his brothers' faults so that his brothers could correct their behaviors.

If Joseph had also thought from his brothers' viewpoint, he might have sought wiser and more peaceful methods to deal with the situation. But he had some self-righteousness, thinking he was right. He couldn't really think from his brothers' standpoints.

One day, Joseph had two unusual dreams. In the first dream, he was binding the sheaves in the field, and the sheaves bound by his brothers bowed down before his sheaf. In the second dream, the sun and the moon and 11 stars bowed down to him (Genesis 37:6-9).

These dreams obviously meant Joseph would become such a noble person that his parents and brothers would honor him. They were God-given dreams. Why did God give him such dreams? It was to show that God would fulfill His will through Joseph. Showing those dreams was a part of God's plan to fulfill His covenant that He had made with Abraham, Isaac, and Jacob.

Since he had those dreams, he had to go through many trials: he was sold as a slave into Egypt and was imprisoned due to groundless accusations. Yet he overcame the hardships every time by remembering the dreams God had given him.

When he was 17, Joseph bragged about his dream before his father and brothers. His brothers were offended because they thought Joseph was looking down on them. Joseph actually had some desire to boast, and he was also short of broad heart to consider other people's standpoints. He quickly bragged about his dreams, and this caused his brothers to hate him. When such jealousy and hatred was piled up, his brothers sold him as a slave to the hands of the Midianite merchants (Genesis 37:28).

Joseph had grown in great favor of his father, but he became a slave overnight. It was a trial of blessing allowed by God for him to demolish his self-righteousness and self-centered frameworks. It was the shortcut for him to reach the level of goodness that God wanted him to have.

After being sold to the merchants, he was then sold to Potiphar, the captain of the bodyguard in Egypt (Genesis 37:36). Now, what kind of attitude do you think Joseph had? Did he give up everything because he was disheartened? Or did he complain about the hardships he was facing? Or did he try to get out of the situation the best he could? He didn't do any of the above.

He just accepted all the circumstances. He thought about why such situations came upon him and he admitted his shortcomings. Witnessing his brothers sell him as a slave, he felt deep in his bones how much they hated him, and why they hated him. He realized that they resented him when he made reports of their faults to their father, and that they were very offended when he was bragging about his dreams. He realized he had thought he was doing the right thing, but actually his brothers were suffering. He repented of all his past wrongdoings.

Joseph knew that his situations couldn't turn around with men's power and methods. He already heard how his father, Jacob, had demolished his self-righteousness at Jabbok River and how he had been reconciled to his brother, Esau. He knew all life's problems are actually in the hands of God. He knew all life's problems are actually in the hands of God. So, he also knew it was only God who could solve his problems, and he committed every matter into God's hands.

Joseph committed everything into God's hands because he believed God was with him and protected him. He still had some self-righteousness remaining in him, but he always listened to God's words and tried to put them into practice. So, even though he was a mere slave now, he had the conviction that God would keep him and guide him. He was at peace because he left everything to God.

It was not because Joseph had some great evil in him that God allowed trials to come upon him. He learned about God from his father since his childhood, and he kept his father's teachings in mind and practiced them. Nevertheless, God still allowed him trials. It was to let him demolish his self-righteousness and to change him into a big vessel to fulfill God's providence.

If a person suffers from retribution caused by his/her sins or goes through trials allowed to cast off great evil from his/her heart, God would turn His face away from them. When they feel completely alone and isolated in trials, they can cast away the evil that has been hardened in their heart. Naturally, these trials are very difficult. For this reason, some people who have a great deal of evil in them give out more evil while they go through those trials, thereby bringing more pain and hardships upon themselves.

But Joseph did not have such great evil. Neither did he complain or reveal evil natures during his trials. He just accepted everything with humbleness and thanksgiving. He feared God unchangingly and lived by His words. Accordingly, God was with him and made him prosperous even during his trials.

After Joseph was sold into Egypt, he caught the eye of Potiphar, his master. It was not simply because Joseph was hardworking and faithful in his duties, but also because of God's intervention. Potiphar chose Joseph to stay close to him because God moved his heart that way. The passage says, "And he was in the house of his master," and it means he stayed near the place where his master was staying.

In ancient times, the lodging of the master and the servants were separated, but Joseph was so trusted that he could stay near his master's bedroom. It proves that Joseph was in great favor of God. People around him witnessed his prosperity and also saw the evidence that God was with him. It is just as the passage says, "Now his master saw that the LORD was with him and how the LORD caused all that he did to prosper in his hand."

Then, how did Potiphar, an Egyptian man who did not serve God the LORD or know about Him, come to acknowledge that God the LORD was with Joseph? We can understand that Joseph preached about the almighty God whom he believed in so that such a man Potiphar acknowledged God was with Joseph.

Whenever Joseph earned praises and received compliments, he gave glory to God. He said he was speaking and acting only according to God's words, and he was prosperous in all things thanks to God's help. At first, Potiphar could have just ignored what Joseph was saying. But as Joseph was prosperous in all things, Potiphar naturally came to acknowledge that God was helping Joseph.

When God caused all that Joseph did to prosper, Joseph did not neglect any of his tasks. It doesn't mean Joseph didn't do what he was supposed to be doing. He faithfully carried out all his duties and tried to measure his master's will and served his master exactly the way his master wanted. He obeyed the will of his master, and the results of his work pleased his master.

2. Being in Charge of Whole Household of Potiphar

So Joseph found favor in his sight and became his personal servant; and he made him overseer over his house, and all that he owned he put in his charge. It came about that from the time he made him overseer in his house and over all that he owned, the LORD blessed the Egyptian's house on account of Joseph; thus the LORD's blessing was upon all that he owned, in the house and in the field. So he left everything he owned in Joseph's charge; and with him there he did not concern himself with anything except the food which he ate. Now Joseph was handsome in form and appearance. (39:4-6)

Though he was a slave, Joseph did not complain but only served his master with his best efforts. The passage says, "So Joseph found favor in his sight and became his personal servant." This tells us Joseph served his master with all his heart. If he had compared his current situation with that of his childhood during which he had received sufficient love from his father Jacob, he could have complained or been disheartened. Also, he could have just done his job feeling forced, thinking it was hard. But he didn't. He was grateful to Potiphar who accepted him, so he served and honored his master with the desire to pay back the grace he had received.

Here, we can see the comparison of the hearts of Jacob and Joseph. Jacob stole the blessings from Esau that had been intended for the firstborn. He fled from Esau and lived in his uncle Laban's house, but he was not thankful there. He didn't have good feelings toward Laban because Laban cheated him and changed his wages many times. But what if Jacob perceived the situation from a different angle? He should have been thankful to Laban because his uncle accepted him when he had nobody to turn to. Furthermore, he gave Jacob his daughters so Jacob could have a family. If Jacob had been thankful to Laban all the time, his trials would have ended sooner.

When they go through hardships, some people get disheartened or fall into despair saying 'old times were good.' They resent and complain about the current situation. They lose strength and give up on their duties. This shows they are narrow-minded and they lack goodness in their heart.

On the contrary those who are good-hearted do not complain even though their current situations are significantly worse than those of the past. They'd only give thanks thinking that in the past they were able to enjoy many things by the grace of God. They can give thanks because, in comparison, they realize the value of the things they used to enjoy.

Joseph accepted the circumstances in his good heart and deeply gave thanks for the things he once enjoyed in the past. Also, his attitude of service toward Potiphar did not change even with the passage of time.

Usually, people work hard until they are recognized or acknowledged, but once they are recognized, many people's attitudes change. But Joseph was unchangingly humble, honest, and faithful. As a result, he was trusted even more than before. He was even put in charge of every matter of his master's household.

Joseph caught the eye of Potiphar by God's work, but Potiphar also saw the integrity and faithfulness of Joseph. As the manager of all the assets of the captain of the bodyguard of the Pharaoh of Egypt, Joseph could have such a great authority. Although he was a slave, Joseph's position in his household was second only to his master.

Just because we are recognized in a certain area, we should not do our duties in a way of eyeservice nor should we neglect them. You have to take care of and be responsible for more things as your position becomes higher. Even if you have currently sat at the higher position than before, you should not forget the grace you received from your superiors (Ephesians 6:5-8). If you serve everybody the way you serve the Lord, you can be recognized and loved by others just like Joseph

(Colossians 3:22-23).

Since the time Potiphar put Joseph in charge of every matter in his household, God blessed Potiphar. God's blessings came upon him even though he did not believe in or serve God. Does this mean Potiphar was blessed solely because of Joseph?

Herein lies the justice of God. Seeing Joseph prosper, Potiphar acknowledged God, and he also knew the blessings came from God. This point was reckoned as goodness by God.

If Potiphar had not acknowledged the God who was with Joseph or the fact that blessings came from God, God couldn't have blessed his household but only Joseph personally.

Suppose there is a person who loves God and is loved by Him very much. God's blessing might come upon the whole family or it might also come only upon that person individually. If the family members deserve to receive the blessings together, they will. Otherwise, only that individual who is loved by God will be blessed.

Potiphar trusted Joseph to an extent that he left everything to Joseph, and did not concern himself with anything except the food he ate. Just by considering this fact we can understand God blessed and guaranteed Joseph so much that it was clearly visible to people. As the captain of the bodyguard in Egypt, Potiphar must have had so much wealth. If he had a single shred of doubt in Joseph, he'd have intervened in many ways. But he received so much blessing thanks to Joseph that he did not have to concern himself with any matter of the household.

Because Joseph demolished his ego and self-righteousness completely, he did not try to insist on his opinions at all. He did not become arrogant just because his position was elevated. He just served his master and obeyed his will with the same heart of service. How trustworthy Joseph must have been in the sight of Potiphar!

In addition to Joseph and his master Potiphar, everyone else in the household could enjoy the blessings together. In the lowly position of a slave, Joseph quickly cast away the attribute of boastful pride and his self-righteousness that had caused him to insist on his opinions.

At the same time, he also equipped himself with the qualifications to become the prime minister of the great ancient Egypt. Being the manager of the whole estate of the captain of the bodyguard, he acquired the ability to manage various matters, which was necessary for his future ministry to manage the whole land of Egypt. Moreover, dealing with various kinds people, he learned the ways to discern the characters and manage human resources, too.

3. Refusing the Seduction of Potiphar's Wife

It came about after these events that his master's wife looked with desire at Joseph, and she said, "Lie with me." But he refused and said to his master's wife, "Behold, with me here, my master does not concern himself with anything in the house, and he has put all that he owns in my charge. There is no one greater in this house than I, and he has withheld nothing from me except you, because you are his wife. How then could I do this great evil and sin against God?" As she spoke to Joseph day after day, he did not listen to her to lie beside her or be with her. (Genesis 39:7-10)

After Joseph learned everything he needed at Potiphar's house, God guided him to the next level. God wanted him to get practical knowledge necessary to the prime minister of Egypt. We might think God could have put Joseph in the royal palace, at the center of the politics. But it was not in accordance with justice for a slave to become a government official and work in the royal palace. God does not go against justice and order.

Suppose a little child is praying with faith to become the president of the country. God cannot make him the president immediately. If this child is praying with true faith, God would guide him in each step of his life so that he can learn and acquire everything necessary to become a good president. When he actually has the qualifications to be the president, God will answer his prayer.

In the same way, God did not elect Joseph as the prime minister immediately. He let him take necessary steps. That process seemed to be a continuation of troubles, but it was the quickest way in God's wisdom and plan. And Potiphar's wife was used as an instrument to open that way for Joseph.

It does not mean, however, that God moved her heart to act in the way she did. Just as Pharaoh was used as an instrument to stand against Moses due to his evil, Potiphar's wife was used as an instrument to seduce Joseph due to her own lust. She became an evil instrument on her own.

Joseph was handsome in form and appearance. Potiphar's wife was drawn by his handsomeness and tried to seduce him. She looked with desire at Joseph, and she said, "Lie with me." Joseph refused saying, "How then could I do this great evil and sin against God?"

But she did not give up. She tried to seduce him every single day. Joseph did not have any desire to commit sins because he had a reverent fear of God. Furthermore, he found favor in his master's eyes very much. His master trusted him so much that he even put him in charge of every matter of his household.

If he slept with his master's wife, it would turn out to be a betrayal to his master, forsaking all the grace he had received. Joseph couldn't just do such a thing. He didn't only refuse the seduction of his master's wife but he wouldn't be anywhere near her. He didn't give her any chance.

Suppose you put yourself in the same shoes. If you do not have any desire to sin, you'd act in the same way that Joseph did. But some want others to seduce them in their heart. Or they do not avoid even in a situation that they can avoid and then commit immoral sins. After committing sins that way, they give excuses saying, "I couldn't help it because the other person was seducing me."

God searches the heart of people. Therefore, we must not give excuses putting the blame on the situation or other people. We have to see through our own hearts. If we don't have any desire to sin, God would help us to avoid even unavoidable situations.

Even though Joseph kept on refusing, Potiphar's wife became even more obsessed. If she had any goodness in her heart, she would be ashamed by Joseph's continuous refusal and regretted her actions. But she showed even greater evil because her lust was burning.

4. Wrongfully Accused by Potiphar's Wife

Now it happened one day that he went into the house to do his work, and none of the men of the household was there inside. She caught him by his garment, saying, "Lie with me!" And he left his garment in her hand and fled, and went outside. When she saw that he had left his garment in her hand and had fled outside, she called to the men of her household and said to them, "See, he has brought in a Hebrew to us to make sport of us; he came in to me to lie with me, and I screamed. When he heard that I raised my voice and screamed, he left his garment beside me and fled and went outside." So she left his garment beside her until his master came home. Then she spoke to him with these words, "The Hebrew slave, whom you brought to us, came in to me to make sport of me; and as I raised my voice and screamed, he left his garment beside me and fled outside." (39:11-18)

One day Joseph went into the house to do his work, and none of the men of the household was there inside. God allowed such a situation to take place because He knew Joseph would never do any evil and it was to guide him to the way to become the prime minister of Egypt by causing all things to work for good.

Potiphar's wife asked Joseph to lie with her catching him by his clothes. There was nobody in the house and it was an opportunity of life time for her. What do you think Joseph's heart was like at that moment? Would he have thought, 'There is no one in the house, and since she is asking so much, maybe I'll just grant her wish just this time' or 'How can I refuse her in this kind of situation'?

Joseph didn't have such an idea at all. When she caught him by his garment he just left his garment in her hand and ran outside. He probably knew he could be in great trouble by doing so. Fundamentally, if one doesn't have any sinful nature in him, he does not compromise with temptations of sin in any situation. Such a person doesn't commit sins at all even though it seems to bring great wealth and social power on him.

Now, Potiphar's wife held grudges against Joseph. She called to the men of her household and wrongfully accused Joseph. She said Joseph came in and tried to lie with her, so she screamed, and then he left his garment beside her and went outside. Joseph's garment in her hand was the 'smoking gun' and it looked like she was telling the truth—Joseph was on the verge of being branded as a sex offender.

When Potiphar got back home he heard shocking news from his wife, which was that Joseph tried to rape her when nobody was around. Moreover, she had Joseph's garment in her hand, which he had left in fleeing the scene.

If Potiphar's wife had had just a little bit of goodness in conscience, she'd have tried to wrap up the incident as quietly as possible. But because she couldn't satisfy her lust, she framed Joseph for rape out of her spite.

If Joseph had had evil mind, he could have defended himself and revealed the fault of the woman. But Joseph considered his master's standpoint and protected her. He just waited for her to realize her fault and back off. And yet she just wrongfully accused Joseph.

5. Imprisoned in God's Providence

Now when his master heard the words of his wife, which she spoke to him, saying, "This is what your slave did to me," his anger burned. So Joseph's master took him and put him into the jail, the place where the king's prisoners were confined; and he was there in the jail. But the LORD was with Joseph and extended kindness to him, and gave him favor in the sight of the chief jailer. The chief jailer committed to Joseph's charge all the prisoners who were in the jail; so that whatever was done there, he was responsible for it. The chief jailer did not supervise anything under Joseph's charge because the LORD was with him; and whatever he did, the LORD made to prosper. (39:19-23)

Potiphar was very angry when he heard what his wife said. He just put Joseph into the jail for the king's prisoners without investigating the incident further or hearing from Joseph. He was even angrier because he felt betrayed by Joseph whom he had trusted very much. He actually loved Joseph and gave him many things. That is why he did not send Joseph to an ordinary jail, but to a jail meant for king's prisoners who committed treason or crimes of disobedience to the king.

Potiphar had fleshly love. With fleshly love, one would want to receive back as much as he has given to the other person. When they feel they are not getting back in return as much as they want, their love could easily turn into hatred. Potiphar was a relatively good person, but he belonged to fleshly goodness, which had a certain limit.

Even though he was so wrongfully accused, Joseph didn't try to defend himself. People must have thought he was a heinous criminal who repaid his master's grace with evil, but he just believed in God who knows everything. He did not try to explain himself or reason with his master's wife. He just committed everything in God's hands and tried to look for the good will of God in allowing him such trials.

Going through the process of being sold as a slave and being imprisoned, Joseph cultivated endurance. He became enabled to see everything in the eyes of goodness and accept everything with thanksgiving.

Joseph was enjoying a comfortable and stable life as the estate manager of Potiphar, but he was put into jail overnight. It was a tremendous ordeal for him in physical sense. It seemed that everything he had worked for collapsed in a moment. But actually, it was the quickest way for him to be eligible to fulfill the duty of the prime minister of Egypt. It was the shortcut for him to be directly connected to the king later.

The reason why God refined Joseph this way was because He trusted him. People are affected by their circumstances and education, as well as they are affected by their parents. If Joseph would be influenced negatively in the jail, God wouldn't have guided him there.

In the prison, Joseph saw and heard so much of evil schemes, playing both sides against the middle, and untruths, but he was never influenced by those things. But rather such experiences served as a chance for him to gain discernment of various things. Because Joseph had already cast away evil from his heart through the trials, there was no chance for the lust of the flesh, the lust of the eyes, and the boastful pride of life to come into him.

He who has already cultivated his heart with the truth won't be affected even under circumstances that are full of untruths. Joseph had upright mind and true faith in the sight of God. He never committed sins before God even though nobody was watching him. He gave thanks to God not only in favorable situations but also in unfavorable ones. Because he walked in the Light, God was with him and extended kindness to him.

Proverbs 16:7 says, *"When a man's ways are pleasing to the LORD, He makes even his enemies to be at peace with him."* Because Joseph pleased God, He let Joseph find favor in the chief jailer's eyes. A chief jailer is equivalent to a warden today.

Joseph was taught the words of God since childhood, and he was upright in all his behaviors. As he gained experiences in Potiphar's household, all his words and manners and attitudes toward people were loveable. He was meticulous in his work. He was intelligent enough to understand more than what he was taught. Chief jailer put Joseph in charge of all the matters of the jail and did not have to supervise anything under Joseph's charge.

Through the process of being sold as a slave into Egypt, Joseph had deeply realized why he had been hated by his brothers. For this reason he tried to humble himself and serve others, especially when his position became higher. He did not just pretend to be serving; he wholeheartedly humbled himself and served others. He served not only his superiors but also his colleagues and subordinates, so he was respected and loved by everyone.

To Egyptians, Joseph was a foreigner. Especially, because he was a slave, when he was put in charge of everything in his master's household, others probably could feel threatened or jealous. But Joseph was not envied but only loved. The same can be said even when he was in jail.

If he had showed just a little bit of conceit or fault, the prisoners wouldn't have listened to him. They probably wouldn't have liked the fact that a fellow prisoner was managing them. But Joseph was loved and recognized by everyone because he served everybody.

When God allows trials, there always is a reason for it. When we realize that reason and change into a person that God wants us to be, the trial will end soon and He will give us comfort and blessings.

Joseph passed the trials very quickly. He thought about why such trials were allowed to him and quickly demolished his self-righteousness and self-centered frameworks. He became a broad-hearted person who could understand other people's hearts and standpoints. That is why both Potiphar and the chief jailer didn't have to supervise what was under Joseph's charge.

A leader cannot lead an organization well only by physical power. There are many kinds of people, and many kinds of situations arise. To work things out properly in all situations, the leader needs to have wisdom of goodness, broad-mindedness, and a great deal of endurance to understand each one's heart and standpoint. Joseph cultivated such attributes in a short period of time.

At the same time, as he was in the jail meant for prisoners of the king, he learned about the manners and rules in the royal palace, and a wide range of viewpoints and knowledge related with the law and administration of the country. Through these trials, he was being changed into the kind of person that God wanted, both physically and spiritually.

… Add-in 1

The God of Abraham, the God Isaac, and the God of Jacob

Abraham, great-grandfather of Joseph and the father of faith, begot Isaac at the age of 100 and lived up to the age of 175. Isaac begot Jacob at the age of 60 and died at the age of 180 (Genesis 35:28-29).

Joseph was sold into Egypt at age 17 and became the prime minister there at age 30. He met his brothers again after the seven years of good harvest and in the second year of famine that followed. When Jacob met Joseph again in 22 years, Joseph was 39 years old and Jacob was 130 (Genesis 41:46, 45:6, 47:9). Jacob lived in Egypt for 17 more years and died at age 147 (Genesis 47:28).

Isaac was 60 years older than Jacob (Genesis 25:26), so when Jacob heard the false report that Joseph was torn by a wild animal, Isaac was also alive.

When his father, Jacob, and grandfather, Isaac, were in despair, Joseph was alone in the foreign country of Egypt. But he did not lose heart even in trials. The dreams given by God and the knowledge of God he acquired from his ancestors served as his support. He knew well about the wonderful God who fulfilled His providence through

Abraham, Isaac, and Jacob. With this knowledge, he firmly believed even in trials that there must be God's good will in his life.

God was with Abraham, Joseph's Great-grandfather

In Genesis 12:1-3, God said to Abram, who was 75 years old, *"Go forth from your country, and from your relatives and from your father's house, to the land which I will show you; and I will make you a great nation, and I will bless you, and make your name great; and so you shall be a blessing."* God wanted to protect Abram from the idolatry that was prevalent in the area where he was living. It was also a part of God's plan to establish him as the father of faith.

Abram believed in the faithful God and obeyed His command immediately without utilizing his own thoughts at all. He was named 'Abraham', (which means "father of a multitude of nations") at age 99 and begot Isaac at age 100, an age at which it was almost impossible to have a child. He also passed the test of faith to give his only son Isaac as a burnt offering. He became a blessing and was called the 'father of faith' and the friend of God.

Joseph heard much about the God who guided the life of Abraham, his great grandfather, and he kept it in mind. So, even when he was sold as a slave into Egypt and put into dire situations, he overcame with faith remembering his great-grandfather.

God was with Isaac, Joseph's Grandfather

Isaac was a nomad. According to the season he went to Gerar and used the wells dug by Abraham. Then, the herdsmen of Gerar quarreled with herdsmen of Isaac saying the wells belonged to them. Isaac just let them keep the wells (Genesis 26:17-22).

Isaac could yield to the herdsmen of Gerar without quarreling with them by the spiritual influence of his father, Abraham. Isaac also tried to imitate Abraham as recorded in Genesis 13:9, which reads, *"Please separate from me; if to the left, then I will go to the right; or if to the right, then I will go to the left."*

Isaac passed those difficult situations with goodness and maintained peace with people around him. For this reason God gave him a word of blessing—prosperity of his descendants (Genesis 26:23-25). Joseph also heard much about God who blessed his grandfather, Isaac. When he was wrongfully accused and put in jail without a cause, he believed God would lead him to the way of blessings and acted in goodness.

God was with Jacob, Joseph's Father

Jacob received the birthright by cheating his brother Esau and his father Isaac. Esau wanted to kill him for that, and so he had to flee and live in a distant place for 20 years. When the time came, he headed back to his home country by the command of God, but his brother Esau was waiting for him along with 400 men, having the intention to kill him.

Jacob realized he couldn't get away from that situation with his own wisdom or methods, and he prayed to God until the socket of his thigh was dislocated at Jabbok River. Finally, by the work of God he was dramatically reconciled with his brother. Joseph witnessed the reconciliation between Jacob and Esau, though he was very young at that time.

Joseph heard about this event in much more detail from his father while he was growing up. He also learned that every matter of the world is in the hands of God. When he had nobody to rely on in a foreign country, Joseph relied on God remembering the lives of his father, grandfather, and great-grandfather.

Joseph remembered that Jacob, Isaac, and Abraham experienced great turns of events in their lives by completely relying on God and he applied this principle in his life as well. He did his best in each day of his life with expectations for the future and looking forward to the guidance of God, who had given him hope through two spiritual dreams.

Joseph
Chapter 2

Interpreting the Dreams of the Cupbearer and the Baker

Joseph Serves the Two Officials in Jail

Two Officials Get Concerned Over Their Dreams

Joseph Interprets the Two Officials' Dreams

Chief Cupbearer Forgets Joseph's Request

1. Joseph Serves the Two Officials in Jail

Then it came about after these things, the cupbearer and the baker for the king of Egypt offended their lord, the king of Egypt. Pharaoh was furious with his two officials, the chief cupbearer and the chief baker. So he put them in confinement in the house of the captain of the bodyguard, in the jail, the same place where Joseph was imprisoned. The captain of the bodyguard put Joseph in charge of them, and he took care of them; and they were in confinement for some time. (40:1-4)

In the ancient Egypt the Pharaoh was considered a representative of god or a demigod. The Pharaoh was a king and his words were the law itself. One day the chief cupbearer and the chief baker for the Pharaoh aroused his anger. They were put in jail which was in the house of the captain of the bodyguard, where Joseph had already been confined.

This was not coincidence. God knew exactly when the two officials would cause the anger of the king, and God worked in a way that Joseph and those two officials would meet each other.

That does not mean God put those officials into jail though they were innocent. They actually did something wrong that would put them into jail. But it's just that the timing was coordinated by God in His plan.

God sticks to the law of justice. He controls all the situations according to the timing and flow of things without a single error. What He harbors in heart will be done as it is harbored and it is never contrary to the law of justice.

Potiphar put Joseph in charge of the important duty to take care of the officials of the king, because he knew what kind of person Joseph was. He put Joseph in charge of them to take care of them. He knew how Joseph had served him with all his heart and mind. He knew Joseph was wise and he served his superiors understanding their intentions.

At first, he was angry when he heard his wife's words and just put Joseph in jail without investigating the case further. But as time went by, good thoughts about Joseph that he used to have were coming back to him. It's because he couldn't find anyone who served his superiors with all their heart as Joseph had done.

The chief cupbearer and the chief baker for the king were both sent to the jail in the house of Potiphar. Potiphar could not treat them lightly since, in many cases in politics, people may seem to have lost their power, but they may recover it in a moment. You could never tell when those two officials would be reinstated.

Potiphar needed a person to take care of them and serve them, and Joseph was the right person. He might have had some hard-feelings against Joseph, but he couldn't deny the fact that Joseph was the only one to whom he could entrust such an important job. From this, we can see that Potiphar could draw a line between official and personal matters, and that Joseph was acknowledged by his master very much.

Of course, it was God who moved the heart of Potiphar to put Joseph in charge of and serve the two officials. But it doesn't mean God forced Potiphar's heart; it just means God moved the good part of Potiphar's heart. God does not force evil people to do good work or to force good people to do evil things.

2. Two Officials Get Concerned Over Their Dreams

Then the cupbearer and the baker for the king of Egypt, who were confined in jail, both had a dream the same night, each man with his own dream and each dream with its own interpretation. When Joseph came to them in the morning and observed them, behold, they were dejected. He asked Pharaoh's officials who were with him in confinement in his master's house, "Why are your faces so sad today?" Then they said to him, "We have had a dream and there is no one to interpret it." Then Joseph said to them, "Do not interpretations belong to God? Tell it to me, please." (40:5-8)

After some time, God showed different dreams to the chief cupbearer and the chief baker. The two dreams showed their different future. Of course, God doesn't indiscriminately show good dreams or bad dreams to random persons. Yes, both of them were in jail because they aroused the anger of the king. But God knew precisely what kinds of lives they had lived. He knew which one would be reinstated and which one would be put to death, and He showed different dreams to each person accordingly.

When Joseph came to see them in the morning they were dejected. He asked them why their faces were so sad. Joseph didn't serve his superiors in pretense but with all his heart and mind. He always thought about what they needed and he watched their countenance all the time. It wasn't to see how the wind blew with them but to make them as comfortable as possible.

The two officials felt Joseph's service was genuine, and that is why they could immediately tell him their dreams. If they had no trust in Joseph, they wouldn't have been able to talk so freely about their dreams. It shows us they could confide in him within a very short period of time. It means Joseph acted in a very trustworthy way before the officials.

In this way, Joseph was recognized and loved by all the people around him wherever he was. This is a desirable life of a Christian who gives out the aroma of Christ. If the officials hadn't trusted Joseph, they probably would have ignored him thinking he could never interpret such dreams. But they quickly told him their dreams.

Here, Joseph didn't interpret the dreams at his discretion. When the two officials said there was nobody to interpret their dreams, he said to them, "Do not interpretations belong to God?" He didn't say he could interpret the dreams on his own. He humbly said God is almighty and interpretations belong to God. He actually interpreted the dreams through the wisdom and inspiration given by God.

When we have a dream or hear about another person's dream, we shouldn't try to interpret them at our discretion. Otherwise, it will only lead to misinterpretation. We shouldn't interpret it with ulterior motives either. Also, we shouldn't be proud just because our interpretations were correct once or twice. In regard to interpreting dreams, we first have to discern whether it's a dream given by God or Satan or coming from our own thoughts. And concerning a dream given by God, we should be able to interpret it correctly by the works of the Holy Spirit.

1 Corinthians 2:13 says, *"which things we also speak, not in words taught by human wisdom, but in those taught by the Spirit, combining spiritual thoughts with spiritual words."* When visions or dreams are interpreted spiritually and correctly, we will have joy and refreshing sensation in our heart. It is the same when we interpret the Scriptures as recorded in 2 Timothy 3:16. We can get correct interpretation with the understanding of God's heart and will by the inspiration of the Holy Spirit. Only then, will our spiritual thirst be quenched and the listeners of our messages feel the fervent works of the Holy Spirit.

3. Joseph Interprets the Two Officials' Dreams

So the chief cupbearer told his dream to Joseph, and said to him, "In my dream, behold, there was a vine in front of me; and on the vine were three branches. And as it was budding, its blossoms came out, and its clusters produced ripe grapes. Now Pharaoh's cup was in my hand; so I took the grapes and squeezed them into Pharaoh's cup, and I put the cup into Pharaoh's hand." Then Joseph said to him, "This is the interpretation of it: the three branches are three days; within three more days Pharaoh will lift up your head and restore you to your office; and you will put Pharaoh's cup into his hand according to your former custom when you were his cupbearer. Only keep me in mind when it goes well with you, and please do me a kindness by mentioning me to Pharaoh and get me out of this house. For I was in fact kidnapped from the land of the Hebrews, and even here I have done nothing that they should have put me into the dungeon." When the chief baker saw that he had interpreted favorably, he said to Joseph, "I also saw in my dream, and behold, there were three baskets of white bread on my head; and in the top basket there were some of all sorts of baked food for Pharaoh, and the birds were eating them out of the basket on my head." Then Joseph answered and said, "This is its interpretation: the three baskets are three days; within three more days Pharaoh will lift up your head from you and will hang you on a tree, and the birds will eat your flesh off you." (40:9-19)

First, the chief cupbearer told his dream to Joseph. In his dream, there was a vine with three branches. It was budding, and its blossoms came out, and its clusters produced ripe grapes. He took the grapes, squeezed them into Pharaoh's cup and put the cup into his hand.

As soon as he heard the dream Joseph gave him the interpretation. The three branches meant three days, and because he squeezed the grapes and served it to Pharaoh, he would be reinstated in three days. It was a very good dream.

After interpreting the dream, Joseph made a request to the cupbearer. He said he had not done anything deserving imprisonment and asked him to mention him to Pharaoh and get him out of the jail. The chief cupbearer cheerfully agreed because he thought he could do anything once he was reinstated.

When Joseph was sold as a slave and when he was put into jail due to groundless accusations, he did not try to get out of his situations. He just believed everything was under God's control, so he did not even try to explain himself and he just protected his master's family.

But that doesn't mean he had no hope for the future. He had the hope that someday a chance might be given to him, and with this attitude he tried his best in his daily life. Now he encountered that chance. He thought that if he was reinstated, the chief cupbearer could get him out of his current situation. It wasn't a chance made by his own efforts, so he believed it was an opportunity given by God.

Now, the chief baker told his dream to Joseph. He saw in his dream, there were three baskets of white bread on his head; and in the top basket there was baked food for Pharaoh, and the birds were eating out of the basket on his head.

Joseph's interpretation was exactly the opposite of the cupbearer's dream. He said the king would behead the baker and hang him on a tree, and the birds would eat his flesh off him in three days.

4. Chief Cupbearer Forgets Joseph's Request

Thus it came about on the third day, which was Pharaoh's birthday that he made a feast for all his servants; and he lifted up the head of the chief cupbearer and the head of the chief baker among his servants. He restored the chief cupbearer to his office, and he put the cup into Pharaoh's hand; but he hanged the chief baker, just as Joseph had interpreted to them. Yet the chief cupbearer did not remember Joseph, but forgot him. (40:20-23)

After three days, it was Pharaoh's birthday and there was a feast. While he was celebrating his birthday with all his servants he called up the chief cupbearer and the chief baker for the king. He restored the chief cupbearer to his office, and he put the cup into Pharaoh's hand; but the chief baker was executed.

It was done just as Joseph had interpreted. But the chief cupbearer forgot about Joseph's request. A month, two months, and even one year passed, but the chief cupbearer did not remember. And again, another year passed.

Now, how did Joseph spend these two years? Did he complain about the chief cupbearer who forgot about him? Was he in despair thinking he had no more hope? That was not the case. He did not lose his faith or hope because he remembered the dream given by God. He did his best in his daily life, giving thanks for all things.

This is the attitude of a person who has true faith. Long time ago, God had given Joseph a promise of blessing through his dream. It seemed things were going the opposite of the dream, but Joseph steadfastly believed in God's promise. Joseph saw that the two officials ended up just as the interpretations of the dreams given by God so that he remembered his dream once again and believed that it would certainly come true.

Even though God has given anyone a promise of blessing, it cannot be fulfilled if the person forsakes the will of God. But if that person faithfully believes in God's promise and follows God's will continuously, it will certainly come true. But in the process of the achievement of the promise, what people think is the right time and that of God could be different from each other. Because Joseph was aware of this fact, he was never disheartened even after two years.

He could have sent a message to the chief cupbearer through the chief jailer. But he never tried to utilize any human method. He just waited for the time of God.

And those two years were a good time of refining for Joseph. God did not let Joseph wait aimlessly for those years. He was waiting for the right timing where every condition would be met.

God could have moved the heart of the chief cupbearer to remember Joseph and get him out of the jail. But it was not the right time yet. What if the cupbearer mentioned Joseph and got him out of the jail immediately he was restored to his office?

Joseph was just a Hebrew slave, and he would have had no chance to go before the Pharaoh. Satisfied with the fact that he was released, probably he would have gone back to his father. Then, all those long years of trials that he had spent in Egypt would have been in vain.

Foreseeing the forthcoming seven years of good harvest and then the seven years of great famine in Egypt, God was opening a way for Joseph to become the prime minister. It doesn't mean God gave good harvest and severe famine in Egypt on purpose to make him the prime minister. As He knew in advance that such things would happen, He was working accordingly.

It was not until the chief cupbearer was reinstated and two more years passed that God caused things to happen in a way that Pharaoh would have a dream and then Joseph would interpret it for him.

Add-in 2

What Kind of Country Was Ancient Egypt?

Egypt is considered one of the four major cradles of ancient civilization. The Egyptian civilization was sophisticated and splendid. How could Egypt have such a sophisticated civilization so early?

Adam's Visits

Before his fall, Adam had the authority to subdue and rule over all things. He governed not only the Garden of Eden but also Earth. Because Earth was under his rule, he made frequent visits to Earth, and whenever he came, he enjoyed beautiful sights at beautiful places. One of the places he visited most often was the Nile and lands around it in today's Egypt. Genesis 2:10 says, *"Now a river flowed out of Eden to water the garden; and from there it divided and became four rivers."* The names of the four rivers were: Pishon, Gihon, Tigris, and Euphrates. And Gihon which flowed around the whole land of Cush was the source of the Nile.

A Cradle of Civilization near the Nile

The Earth became even more beautiful and the lands became fertile as the four big rivers were made, which had its source from Eden. But after Adam's fall and he was driven out of the Garden of Eden, Earth was also cursed and it became increasingly barren (Genesis 3:17-18). Of course, although it was cursed, it was much cleaner and more fertile than now.

Egypt's civilization developed around the Nile, as it is called "The Gift of the Nile". The river used to flood often, and many reservoirs and irrigation facilities were built. Agriculture also developed and the land was economically stable. Egypt became a central place in the ancient Near East, along with Mesopotamia around Euphrates and Tigris.

Splendid Civilization

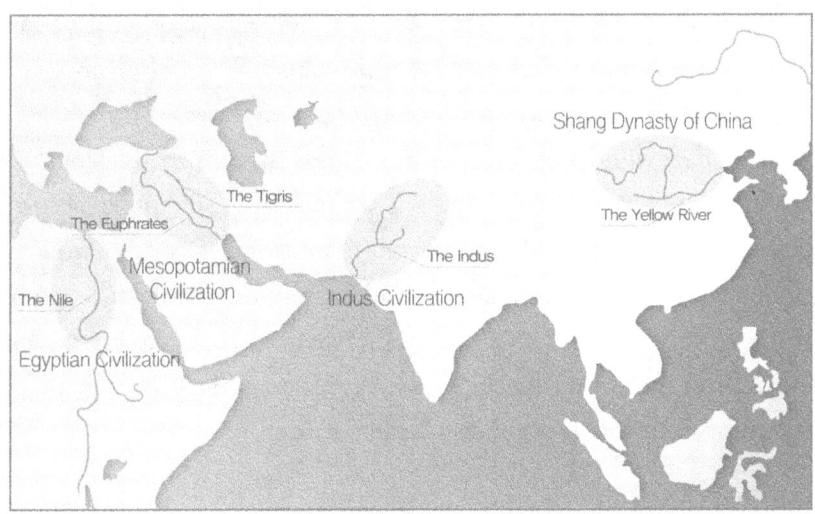

The Four Ancient Civilizations

Egypt has much more sophisticated and splendid remains of civilization than those of the other civilizations. To name a few, the pyramids and the Sphinx are examples. Such amazing remains are also related with the name "Gihon" (Genesis 2:13), which has the meaning "worthy to boast" or "worthy to compare".

At Giza, Egypt, there are two more pyramids near the main pyramid. They have some similarities with the central three stars of the Orion constellation. The third pyramid is a lot smaller than the other two, and the brightness of the third star in Orion is also the least. Also, the third pyramid and the third star are both slightly off the straight line from the other two.

These pyramids were built with such a sophisticated level of construction technology that it's difficult to imitate even with modern technology. There is also amazing astrological and mathematical knowledge contained in the pyramids. The biggest one has 2.3 million pieces of 2.5 ton stones on top of each other. The gap between each stone is less than 0.5 millimeters. We can only imagine what kind of sophisticated technology was used there.

Another wonder of the ancient world is the Sphinx. Its length is about 74 meters and the height is 20 meters. It is one single piece of carved stone. Where did this big stone come from? It is truly a wonder that such structures as pyramids and Sphinx were built such a long time ago in an ancient civilization. But we might begin to grasp such structures if we consider the fact that Adam used to visit this place often while he was living in the Garden of Eden.

Joseph

Chapter 3

The Hebrew Slave, Joseph, Becomes the Prime Minister

Pharaoh has Strange Dreams

The Chief Cupbearer Recommends Joseph

Pharaoh Asks Joseph to Interpret His Dreams

Joseph Suggests Detailed Provisions

In Him is a Divine Spirit: "You Shall Be over My House"

Prime Minister Joseph Prepares for Famine

1. Pharaoh has Strange Dreams

Now it happened at the end of two full years that Pharaoh had a dream, and behold, he was standing by the Nile. And lo, from the Nile there came up seven cows, sleek and fat; and they grazed in the marsh grass. Then behold, seven other cows came up after them from the Nile, ugly and gaunt, and they stood by the other cows on the bank of the Nile. The ugly and gaunt cows ate up the seven sleek and fat cows. Then Pharaoh awoke. He fell asleep and dreamed a second time; and behold, seven ears of grain came up on a single stalk, plump and good. Then behold, seven ears, thin and scorched by the east wind, sprouted up after them. The thin ears swallowed up the seven plump and full ears. Then Pharaoh awoke, and behold, it was a dream. Now in the morning his spirit was troubled, so he sent and called for all the magicians of Egypt, and all its wise men. And Pharaoh told them his dreams, but there was no one who could interpret them to Pharaoh. (41:1-8)

Two years had passed since Joseph interpreted the chief cupbearer's dream and the cupbearer was restored to his office. One day the

Pharaoh had very strange dreams.

It says that he was standing by the Nile. From the Nile came up seven cows, sleek and fat; and they grazed in the marsh grass. Then, seven other cows came up after them from the Nile, ugly and gaunt, and they stood by the other cows on the bank of the Nile. The ugly and gaunt cows ate up the seven sleek and fat cows.

Then he awoke, but then fell asleep again and had another dream. Seven ears of grain came up on a single stalk, plump and good. Then, seven ears, thin and scorched by the east wind, sprouted up after them. The thin ears swallowed up the seven plump and full ears.

The Pharaoh was standing by the Nile, and the Nile symbolizes a "test". Images of a river-side or streams have good meanings because the water represents the Word of God. Thus, 'standing by the Nile' means there will be a test given by God, and the outcome will belong to blessing.

After waking up, Pharaoh felt they were not ordinary dreams. He was very concerned, but there was no way to understand the meanings. He called all the magicians and wise men to interpret them, but nobody could.

In ancient societies, some magicians that worshiped supernatural things conducted rituals. The word "magic" comes from the word "magnus" which referred to the ancient Persian priests who performed religious rituals. They used hypnosis, magic, or power of evil spirits for fortune-telling or to bring down something like a disaster. We can read about the existence of such magicians from the records about the magicians that stood against Moses at the time of Exodus.

But even these people could not interpret the dreams, and Pharaoh was in agony. Now, the cupbearer suddenly remembered a certain individual. It was Joseph who had given him the interpretation for a dream he had had in the jail. He had completely forgotten about it for the past two years. His interaction with Joseph flashed through his mind. He also remembered his promise to Joseph saying that he would mention him to the Pharaoh and get him out of the jail.

When the time of God came, everything was going well as if it was all a part of well thought-out plan. Everything went smoothly in God's providence like it was a stream of water.

2. The Chief Cupbearer Recommends Joseph

Then the chief cupbearer spoke to Pharaoh, saying, "I would make mention today of my own offenses. Pharaoh was furious with his servants, and he put me in confinement in the house of the captain of the bodyguard, both me and the chief baker. We had a dream on the same night, he and I; each of us dreamed according to the interpretation of his own dream. Now a Hebrew youth was with us there, a servant of the captain of the bodyguard, and we related them to him, and he interpreted our dreams for us. To each one he interpreted according to his own dream. And just as he interpreted for us, so it happened; he restored me in my office, but he hanged him." (41:9-13)

Seeing that nobody was able to interpret the Pharaoh's dreams, the chief cupbearer decided to recommend Joseph to the king. But he did not immediately say the name. As if he were talking about something else, he began by saying, "I would make mention today of my own offenses."

He explained about the dream he had when he and the chief baker were in jail. He further explained that a Hebrew youth interpreted their dreams, and just as he had interpreted, he had been restored to his office but the chief baker was hung. He humbled himself by beginning his statement with, "I would make mention today of my own offenses," and he explained how precise Joseph's interpretations were.

Though he did not speak many words, he was very persuasive. Then, why didn't he just recommend Joseph to the king directly but spoke about him indirectly? Here lies his wisdom. This type of speech is more persuasive and convincing.

Suppose the chief cupbearer said, "There is a Hebrew slave named Joseph. I met him when I was in jail. He is good at interpreting dreams, and why don't you call him up to interpret your dreams?" Then, do you suppose that Pharaoh would have listened to him?

Of course, the Pharaoh could have reacted in different ways depending on the extent to which he trusted the cupbearer, but it certainly would not have been enough to draw the king's attention. The king might even have felt uncomfortable and said, "Are you saying a mere Hebrew slave is better than all the magicians and wise men of Egypt? How can he interpret the dreams that those people couldn't?"

Then, that would have been the end of the conversation. The chief cupbearer was wise to make a speech that he made before the Pharaoh so that the king would naturally have interest in Joseph.

God chose this chief cupbearer because He knew his personality and wisdom. He used him as an instrument to connect Joseph with the Pharaoh. While serving the Pharaoh, he gained the experiences and wisdom to be able to persuade the king, and for this reason God used him.

What if the chief cupbearer didn't care about the grace he had received? Even if he remembered Joseph, he didn't have any obligation to recommend Joseph to the king. It'd be OK if Joseph's interpretations were correct, but if not, he was also going to be held responsible.

The chief cupbearer knew he could suffer if Joseph's interpretation was wrong, but he recommended Joseph anyway in order to keep his promise. The reason why he forgot about Joseph for the previous two years is because it was not yet the time for God to move his heart. But when the time came, God let him remember Joseph, and he did not forsake the grace he had once received.

3. Pharaoh Asks Joseph to Interpret His Dreams

Then Pharaoh sent and called for Joseph, and they hurriedly brought him out of the dungeon; and when he had shaved himself and changed his clothes, he came to Pharaoh. Pharaoh said to Joseph, "I have had a dream, but no one can interpret it; and I have heard it said about you, that when you hear a dream you can interpret it." Joseph then answered Pharaoh, saying, "It is not in me; God will give Pharaoh a favorable answer." So Pharaoh spoke to Joseph, "In my dream, behold, I was standing on the bank of the Nile; and behold, seven cows, fat and sleek came up out of the Nile, and they grazed in the marsh grass. Lo, seven other cows came up after them, poor and very ugly and gaunt, such as I had never seen for ugliness in all the land of Egypt; and the lean and ugly cows ate up the first seven fat cows. Yet when they had devoured them, it could not be detected that they had devoured them, for they were just as ugly as before. Then I awoke. I saw also in my dream, and behold, seven ears, full and good, came up on a single stalk; and lo, seven ears, withered, thin, and scorched by the east wind, sprouted up after them; and the thin ears swallowed the seven good ears. Then I told it to the magicians, but there was no one who could explain it to me." Now Joseph said to Pharaoh, "Pharaoh's dreams are one and the same; God has told to Pharaoh what He is about to do. The seven good cows are seven years; and the seven good ears are seven years; the dreams are one and the same. The seven lean and ugly cows that came up after them are seven years, and the seven thin ears scorched by the east wind will be seven years of famine. It is as I have spoken to Pharaoh: God has shown to Pharaoh what He is about to do. Behold, seven years of great abundance are coming in all the land of Egypt; and after them seven years of famine will come, and all the abundance will be forgotten in the land of Egypt, and the famine will ravage the land. So the abundance will be unknown in the land because of that subsequent famine; for it will be very severe." (41:14-31)

The words of the chief cupbearer were like sweet rain to the ears of Pharaoh who had been in agony. Pharaoh quickly sent a man and called up Joseph. Finally, it was the time set by God that Joseph stood before Pharaoh. Pharaoh explained to Joseph there was no one who could interpret his dreams, and said, "I have heard it said about you, that when you hear a dream you can interpret it."

Joseph knew it was God's will that he stood before Pharaoh. So, he was not nervous or afraid when he heard the calling of Pharaoh. He did not think impatiently that his time came. He just answered Pharaoh, "It is not in me; God will give Pharaoh a favorable answer." He was bold even before the king because he was speaking in the name of God.

Also, Joseph certainly believed that everything is in God's hands and the interpretation of the dreams would come from God. That is why he, in a very assuring way, answered Pharaoh that interpretations would come from God. He knew he could interpret Pharaoh's dreams only if God let him know. So, he humbled himself and lifted up the name of God.

As the Pharaoh told him his dreams, Joseph immediately gave him the interpretation. He knew the answer right away because God inspired him. In this way, if you receive the work of God, you wouldn't have to hesitate or try to think it over.

Joseph's interpretations were as extraordinary as the Pharaoh's dreams. Both the seven cows fat and sleek and the seven ears full and good symbolized seven years of abundance. But the seven cows ugly and gaunt and the seven ears withered and thin symbolized seven years of complete famine.

Pharaoh's dreams meant Egypt would have seven years of abundance and seven years of famine would immediately follow. Also, the gaunt cows devouring the sleek cows and the withered ears swallowing the good ears meant the famine would be so severe as to forget the previous abundance.

4. Joseph Suggests Detailed Provisions

Now as for the repeating of the dream to Pharaoh twice, it means that the matter is determined by God, and God will quickly bring it about. Now let Pharaoh look for a man discerning and wise, and set him over the land of Egypt. Let Pharaoh take action to appoint overseers in charge of the land, and let him exact a fifth of the produce of the land of Egypt in the seven years of abundance. Then let them gather all the food of these good years that are coming, and store up the grain for food in the cities under Pharaoh's authority, and let them guard it. Let the food become as a reserve for the land for the seven years of famine which will occur in the land of Egypt, so that the land will not perish during the famine. (41:32-36)

At that time agriculture and ranching were the major industries. Even the strongest nation wouldn't be able to survive seven years of severe famine. It'd be such a great disaster if Joseph's interpretations were to come true.

Pharaoh was surprised hearing the interpretation, and Joseph suggested in detail the provisions they could make for the famine. First, Pharaoh was to set a wise man over the land of Egypt and appoint overseers in charge of the land, so that they could exact a fifth of the produce and store up the grain during the seven years of abundance.

Of course, if you know seven years of famine will follow seven years of abundance, anyone can say you want to store up the harvest during the seven years to prepare for the next seven years. But Joseph did not just say to store up some harvest to prepare for the famine. He came up with a specific number as to how much grain to store.

What if the Pharaoh was to ask his servants to come up with a plan? First, they would have had to calculate average harvest of the whole nation and how much grain was necessary to feed the whole population. Then, they would have to estimate the amounts of harvest for the years of abundance and then those of famine.

They would have to calculate what the amount of grain would be needed for food, animals' feed, and the seeds. There were just so many things to consider and calculate. Even if they finished calculating everything, one could not easily draw a conclusion on different topics making the provisions for the famine. There could be many unexpected factors even if they thought of all the possible scenarios.

But Joseph without any hesitation suggested the number, a fifth of the produce. Of course, it was possible because God gave him wisdom, but it also tells us the fact that he was very familiar with the economy of Egypt as a whole.

He was in charge of a big economy as the manager of the whole estate of the captain of the bodyguard. He was a capable man. He didn't have just some knowledge or information in the brain but he had hands-on experience of real economic matters. Furthermore, he was well acquainted with the economy of the country because, while he was in jail, he heard and learned many things regarding the politics and economy of the country.

He received the inspiration of God when he was already prepared, and so he could immediately come up with the specific plans to deal with the problem. This is one of the reasons why God tried Joseph in Potiphar's house and then in jail. God guided him in a way that he would be equipped both in spiritual and physical aspects.

5. In Him is a Divine Spirit: "You Shall Be over My House"

Now the proposal seemed good to Pharaoh and to all his servants. Then Pharaoh said to his servants, "Can we find a man like this, in whom is a divine spirit?" So Pharaoh said to Joseph, "Since God has informed you of all this, there is no one so discerning and wise as you are. You shall be over my house, and according to your command all my people shall do homage; only in the throne I will be greater than you." Pharaoh said to Joseph, "See, I have set you over all the land of Egypt." Then Pharaoh took off his signet ring from his hand and put it on Joseph's hand, and clothed him in garments of fine linen and put the gold necklace around his neck. He had him ride in his second chariot; and they proclaimed before him, "Bow the knee!" And he set him over all the land of Egypt. Moreover, Pharaoh said to Joseph, "Though I am Pharaoh, yet without your permission no one shall raise his hand or foot in all the land of Egypt." Then Pharaoh named Joseph Zaphenath-paneah; and he gave him Asenath, the daughter of Potiphera priest of On, as his wife. And Joseph went forth over the land of Egypt." (41:37-45)

Pharaoh was very happy with Joseph's proposal that followed the clear interpretation. He felt his mind was refreshed and cleared. He liked Joseph very much because he was wise and humble, and he seemed to be faithful, too.

Not just the king but also his servants liked Joseph's suggestion. Because the interpretation of Joseph was so clear, they could trust him deeply even though they met him for the first time.

Pharaoh was very glad and said, "Can we find a man like this, in whom is a divine spirit?" He acknowledged God was with Joseph and highly appreciated his wisdom and understanding.

In this situation, the ministers could be concerned about the Pharaoh's words. They might have somewhat resented the fact that Pharaoh listened to and trusted a Hebrew slave more than all the ministers of Egypt.

But they didn't. Even when the Pharaoh trusted Joseph and accepted all his suggestions, they didn't resent it, and they were not jealous of Joseph. They didn't look down on Joseph because he was a Hebrew slave. It tells us both Pharaoh and the ministers had good heart and their hearts were united at the moment.

Now, Pharaoh proclaimed Joseph would be over his house. He said he would be higher than Joseph only in the throne, and he took out the signet ring from his hand and put it on Joseph's hand. The Pharaoh's signet ring was made from a stone or metal with an image. It was used to sign the important documents. It symbolized the authority and power of the Pharaoh. Therefore, what Pharaoh did meant Joseph would be in charge of all the administrations of the whole country.

Pharaoh clothed him in garments of fine linen and put the gold necklace around his neck. He had him ride in his second chariot; and they proclaimed before him, "Bow the knee!" And he set him over all the land of Egypt. He said without Joseph's permission no one should raise his hand or foot in all the land of Egypt.

Pharaoh entrusted all his authorities to Joseph to prepare for the seven years of famine. He put him at the position second only to Pharaoh himself. It was a great turn of events for Joseph to become the prime minister of the great nation. He had been sold as a slave from a foreign land, and moreover, he'd been a prisoner. But now was the time that God had planned. It was God's blessing given to Joseph who had passed many trials.

The servants of Pharaoh might have felt the decision was made too abruptly. Overnight, they now had to bow to a person who used to be a Hebrew slave. They could have complained, too.

They might have thought they knew about the situations of Egypt much better than Joseph and tried to get the Pharaoh to revoke his decision. Or, even though they seemed to follow Joseph's plan outwardly, they might have harbored an ulterior motive to get rid of him because they thought they could deal with the problem without Joseph's help. But in reality, none of Pharaoh's servants harbored such evil thoughts.

Of course, Pharaoh was also taking a great risk by putting a Hebrew slave in charge of all the land of Egypt. And yet he did it anyway.

Joseph's dream came true 13 years after he was sold as a slave into Egypt. Pharaoh gave Joseph an Egyptian name 'Zaphenath-paneah,' which means, "God speaks and He is alive."

Pharaoh then gave him Asenath, the daughter of Potiphera priest of On, as his wife. On was the name of a city located at the southern part of the Nile delta. It was a central part in Egypt at that time. Giving Joseph a woman as a wife who was from the family of a priest, which was respected and admired by people, means that Pharaoh treated Joseph in the best ways he could.

When Pharaoh gave Joseph Asenath as his wife, he trusted Joseph not just with words but in deeds. He endowed Joseph with such authority and power that could prevent anybody from looking down on him. Pharaoh showed the fullest extent of consideration for Joseph so that he could rule over Egypt at his will.

Without such support from the Pharaoh, Joseph could have faced many kinds of challenges and difficulties. But with this support of Pharaoh, Joseph could put to use the wisdom given by God to the fullest degree, without any hesitation or reservation. As a result, Joseph did a great favor for Egypt and Pharaoh.

Also, Pharaoh could escape the disaster by making Joseph the prime minister to prepare for the seven years of famine. Without Joseph, Egypt would have been devastated even to the point of no recovery due to the prolonged famine. Therefore, Joseph was the savior for the Egyptian king and the people.

Pharaoh and his country could receive such grace because it was in accordance with the justice of God. It means Pharaoh and his ministers had good hearts. If they had not acknowledged Joseph and if they had not followed Joseph's plan, Egypt wouldn't have been able to countermeasure the great calamity.

It would have been the same if the Pharaoh and his ministers were not in agreement. In his good heart, Pharaoh was moved to follow Joseph's plan, and the ministers also followed his opinion. As a result, the whole country and the people were shown mercy. It is of great importance for the leader and the workers to be united in an organization.

Even today, we can see God's direction and intervention when all the workers in the ministry of God are united as one and have peace. The enemy Satan cannot work among the people whose hearts are united. So, as long as they are not off the track of God's will, everything will go smoothly. However, things will not go well with many talented workers if they are not united and peace is broken. Where there is no peace, Satan begins to work.

The Pharaoh's and the ministers' hearts were in unison, so it was in accordance with God's justice. If Pharaoh's heart had been hardened and the ministers had been jealous of Joseph, God wouldn't have caused them to stay in favor of God. God uses both good vessels and evil vessels according to their qualities.

That doesn't mean Pharaoh and the ministers reached a level of goodness according to God's standard. The levels of goodness that God requires are different for different people.

Pharaoh and the ministers were Gentiles who did not believe in God. And yet, they acknowledged a man of God. This was the act that could be considered goodness. There is also another important point here. It is that, even though you have the level of goodness, love, and faith with which you can receive an answer from God, they'd be useless if you don't obey when God moves your heart to do a certain thing.

For this reason God searches for those who are obedient when He accomplishes His work. God chose and used Pharaoh as an instrument because He knew Pharaoh would trust Joseph's words and follow his plans. If this Pharaoh had the same hardened heart that the Pharaoh at the time of the Exodus did, he wouldn't have been able to acknowledge a man of God.

As explained, when He was planning to fulfill His providence, God considered even the characters of the Pharaoh then, so that He could cause all things to work for good. That is why the timing in God's sight is important.

God's providence will not be fulfilled by forcing people. God knows the exact point in time when everything will be done in perfect harmony, and He does His work precisely at that point. The time of God for Joseph was when he was 30 years old.

6. Prime Minister Joseph Prepares for Famine

Now Joseph was thirty years old when he stood before Pharaoh, king of Egypt. And Joseph went out from the presence of Pharaoh and went through all the land of Egypt. During the seven years of plenty the land brought forth abundantly. So he gathered all the food of these seven years which occurred in the land of Egypt and placed the food in the cities; he placed in every city the food from its own surrounding fields. Thus Joseph stored up grain in great abundance like the sand of the sea, until he stopped measuring it, for it was beyond measure. Now before the year of famine came, two sons were born to Joseph, whom Asenath, the daughter of Potiphera priest of On, bore to him. Joseph named the firstborn Manasseh, "For," he said, "God has made me forget all my trouble and all my father's household." He named the second Ephraim, "For," he said, "God has made me fruitful in the land of my affliction." When the seven years of plenty which had been in the land of Egypt came to an end, and the seven years of famine began to come, just as Joseph had said, then there was famine in all the lands, but in all the land of Egypt there was bread. So when all the land of Egypt was famished, the people cried out to Pharaoh for bread; and Pharaoh said to all the Egyptians, "Go to Joseph; whatever he says to you, you shall do." When the famine was spread over all the face of the earth, then Joseph opened all the storehouses, and sold to the Egyptians; and the famine was severe in the land of Egypt. The people of all the earth came to Egypt to buy grain from Joseph, because the famine was severe in all the earth. (41:46-57)

In the providence of God, Joseph was sold as a slave into Egypt, and at the age of 30 he interpreted Pharaoh's dream and became the prime minister of Egypt. But being a prime minister was far from enjoying his authority and living a comfortable life.

Immediately he began inspecting all the land of Egypt. Both his mind and body were busy in order to prepare for the seven years of abundance and then the seven years of famine. He had to gain wisdom of God as to where to make the storehouses for food, and how they could keep them for a long time without letting the food go bad.

As God gave the interpretation of the dream, Egypt immediately had seven years of abundance. What if they didn't know after the seven years was waiting severe famine of the next seven years? They would have wasted all the abundant harvest that they had gained for seven years. But because Joseph had a plan to prepare for the famine, they gathered a certain amount of food every year and stored them in the cities. The food that was stored was so much that it was like the sand of the sea.

When they were enjoying the joy of abundant harvest, God gave Joseph two sons. We can feel God's delicate love here. Wouldn't it have been better to have the children during the time of abundance rather than during the famine?

Joseph's first son's name, Manasseh, means 'to forget.' Joseph actually forgot about all the trials he had had in the past. His second son's name Ephraim means to be fruitful, and Joseph's hard-work and efforts he had expended in Egypt produced abundant fruit. He received blessings both physically and spiritually without lacking anything.

The seven years of abundance ended and finally the famine started. While the abundance continued for seven years, people might have had some expectation that the abundance would continue as it had been.

Some people might have thought it was a hard work to gather 1/5 of the food and store it in each city (Genesis 41:34-36). Some people might have doubted the fact that famine was coming.

But as the abundance actually came to an end and the famine started, they had to acknowledge Joseph. The famine was not confined to Egypt alone, but it affected other neighboring countries. But thanks to the prime minister Joseph, Egypt stored food during the seven years of abundance, and they had enough food even during the severe famine.

The people of the nearby countries heard about this and came to Egypt to buy food. Joseph successfully dealt with all the hardships with his faithfulness, integrity, and attention to detail that he had shown in Potiphar's household and in the jail.

"I have been here because God has been here.
I give You thanks that,
In the grace and blessing of God,
I have been made honorable
And I have made God known to many people.

God's love has been overwhelming to me.
There was a flood of evidence that God loved me.

I give You thanks that You accomplished
So many things through me,
You have reaped such great fruit,
And You were delighted.

Part 2

*Joseph's Wisdom of Goodness
Saves Israel and Egypt*

Part 2

Jacob's twelve sons are the foundation stones to form the nation of Israel.

As Joseph understood this providence of God, he put in effect his wisdom of goodness so that his brothers could demolish the wall of sins before God and form the twelve tribes of Israel.

It is a deep level of love to save all, going beyond the level of mere forgiving.

Joseph
Chapter 4

"Your Words May Be Tested, Whether There Is Truth in You"

Jacob's Ten Sons Went to Egypt to Buy Grain

"Where Have You Come From? You Are Spies"

Joseph Puts His Brothers in Prison

"If You Are Honest Men, Bring Your Youngest Brother"

Jacob Laments Saying He Will Also Lose Benjamin

1. Jacob's Ten Sons Went to Egypt to Buy Grain

Now Jacob saw that there was grain in Egypt, and Jacob said to his sons, "Why are you staring at one another?" He said, "Behold, I have heard that there is grain in Egypt; go down there and buy some for us from that place, so that we may live and not die." Then ten brothers of Joseph went down to buy grain from Egypt. But Jacob did not send Joseph's brother Benjamin with his brothers, for he said, "I am afraid that harm may befall him." So the sons of Israel came to buy grain among those who were coming, for the famine was in the land of Canaan also. (42:1-5)

While Egypt was having the famine, the land of Canaan where Jacob and his family were living was suffering from severe famine as well. As he took the responsibility for his family, his concerns grew day after day.

Jacob heard there was grain in Egypt. He called his sons and said,

"Why are you staring at one another?" He was making a point to his grown up sons because they didn't take any action to deal with their situation. We can infer from this sentence what kind of relationship Jacob and his sons had. Namely, Jacob did not consider his sons reliable. Also, in the view of the sons, they couldn't take initiative because they knew they were not trusted by their father.

Jacob's sons didn't depart for Egypt until they were told to go and buy some grain. But Jacob didn't send Benjamin with other sons. He thought Joseph died, and all his love went to Benjamin, because Benjamin was born of Rachel whom Jacob had loved the most among the four wives. Jacob was worried that Benjamin might be harmed, and he didn't send him to Egypt.

It tells us it was not easy for them to go to Egypt and buy grain. Because of the severe famine, there could have been thieves, robbers, and other kinds of dangers. Especially, because they were going to a distant country, Jacob was nervous.

So, how did the rest of the sons react to the fact that Benjamin was staying? When Jacob favored Joseph in the past, the other sons felt uncomfortable about it. But they were different now. They had the sense of guilt after they sold Joseph as a slave out of their jealousy. Moreover, Benjamin was much younger than they were, and he was different from Joseph, too.

Joseph used to be condescending toward his brothers because he considered himself smart and because he was loved by his father Jacob. Benjamin, however, had a kind of weak temperament, and he did not say or do anything that could provoke his brothers. He didn't try to lift himself up. Neither did he bring bad reports about his brothers to his father. So, even though Benjamin was favored by their father, his brothers did not hate him. And they didn't find it uncomfortable that Benjamin was excluded from going to Egypt to buy food.

2. "Where Have You Come From? You Are Spies"

Now Joseph was the ruler over the land; he was the one who sold to all the people of the land. And Joseph's brothers came and bowed down to him with their faces to the ground. When Joseph saw his brothers he recognized them, but he disguised himself to them and spoke to them harshly. And he said to them, "Where have you come from?" And they said, "From the land of Canaan, to buy food." But Joseph had recognized his brothers, although they did not recognize him. Joseph remembered the dreams which he had about them, and said to them, "You are spies; you have come to look at the undefended parts of our land." Then they said to him, "No, my lord, but your servants have come to buy food. We are all sons of one man; we are honest men, your servants are not spies." (42:6-11)

Jacob's sons arrived in Egypt. They bowed and paid homage to Joseph who was the prime minister of Egypt. They could never have imagined that Joseph had become the prime minister, and they did not recognize him.

But Joseph always remembered the dreams that God had given him when he was young. He believed he would meet his father and brothers someday. He recognized them as soon as he saw them. What would Joseph have felt meeting his brothers in 20 years? They had tried to kill him and eventually sold him as a slave. Joseph did not hate them, but just had deep affection for them.

Joseph realized his shortcomings and came to understand the standpoints of his brothers while he was going through the trials. He came to put the blame on himself for what had happened to him and thought if he had understood his brothers a little more, they wouldn't have hated him. He understood they could have had peace if he had not been boastful and if he had covered his brothers' faults with love and acceptance. His heart had been changed into beautiful and good heart through the trials.

Joseph's brothers' act was evil, but Joseph held no grudges or resentment. He just had compassion on his brothers, and he was just thankful that God had caused all things to work for good. He strongly wished he could just embrace them with weeping and let his father know that he was alive. But if he had, God's providence couldn't be completely fulfilled. What does this mean?

Jacob's twelve sons were the foundation stones to establish the nation of Israel. But they had a barrier that hindered them from being united as one. It's that they were born of four different mothers and that they had some conflicts among each other due to their father's favoritism. Because of this conflict they even committed an evil act of selling their brother as a slave.

Of course, after selling Joseph, the other brothers had pangs of conscience and felt sorry for their father. But as time went, such feelings faded away as well. It was a dim memory that they didn't really want to talk about.

It was difficult for such brothers to have true love or a spirit of unity among each other. Although the whole family was about to die of hunger due to severe famine, they didn't take any initiative to do something about it until their father brought it up.

In this situation, what if Joseph just forgave them and showed love to them? Their conflicts would remain and they would be unable to be united. They wouldn't deeply realize how evil they had been in the past, so they wouldn't be able to change. If one nation had come forth from them in this state, it would have been difficult for its people to be united.

For this reason, God wanted to give the brothers a chance to completely repent of what they had done to Joseph. Furthermore, He wanted them to love and care for each other through that chance. This chance was given by the love of God who wanted them to repent of all their wrongdoings and have a new start without any blemish.

Joseph was very glad to see his brothers and he wanted to share joy with them. How happy he must have been at the reunion! He really must have liked to hear about his father, too. But he didn't. He was an affectionate person, and his heart was changed into a heart of goodness through the trials.

And yet, he exercised self-control because he put the providence of God ahead of his personal feelings. Following the urging of God, Joseph pretended he did not know them. He asked them with stern words where they were from. Without knowing anything, they said they were from Canaan and they came to buy some food. Then, Joseph accused them saying they were spies who came to spy on Egypt.

They were awfully shocked. If they had recognized Joseph, they must have thought it was payback for what they had done to him. But Joseph didn't have such an intention at all.

Joseph was reminded of his dreams. His brothers' sheaves bowed down to his sheaf, and the sun and the moon and eleven stars bowed down to him. He knew the dreams were given by God and believed they would come true, and behold, his brothers were bowing down to him.

But this was not complete fulfillment of his dreams. His brothers merely bowed down to the prime minster of Egypt to get some food. It doesn't mean they acknowledged the providence of God and bowed down before their younger brother wholeheartedly.

Joseph knew he had to make his brothers submit to God from the bottom of their heart, and that is why he kept on accusing them of being spies. It was not to take revenge or to be honored by them but only to fulfill the providence of God. For the nation of Israel to be formed through them, they had to repent thoroughly and change.

3. Joseph Puts His Brothers in Prison

Yet he said to them, "No, but you have come to look at the undefended parts of our land!" But they said, "Your servants are twelve brothers in all, the sons of one man in the land of Canaan; and behold, the youngest is with our father today, and one is no longer alive." Joseph said to them, "It is as I said to you, you are spies; by this you will be tested: by the life of Pharaoh, you shall not go from this place unless your youngest brother comes here! Send one of you that he may get your brother, while you remain confined, that your words may be tested, whether there is truth in you. But if not, by the life of Pharaoh, surely you are spies." So he put them all together in prison for three days. (42:12-17)

As they were suddenly and groundlessly accused of being spies, Joseph's brothers began to explain their family situation. They intended to prove that they were not spies. Thanks to that Joseph heard the news about his father, Jacob, and his younger brother, Benjamin. He heard that his father was alive and Benjamin was fine, and they were still living in Canaan.

Now, Joseph told his brothers to bring their youngest brother Benjamin to prove their truth. Joseph had a reason for saying this.

Because Benjamin was born of the same mother, it is human nature that Joseph had more love for him. Benjamin was very young when Joseph was sold as a slave. More than 20 years had passed since then, and Joseph must have missed his brother very much. He must have wondered if he had grown up well among the other brothers.

Another reason why Joseph told his brothers to bring Benjamin was to see their reaction. They had sold Joseph as a slave twenty years ago, and he intended to indirectly find out what kind of attitude his brothers had now.

After giving them this instruction, Joseph confined them in prison for three days. It was to give them some time to look back on themselves. And they must have had many thoughts during the three-day confinement.

They had worries, and they also remembered their past wrongdoings one by one. Also, the prime minister of Egypt wouldn't have just spoken meaningless words, so they knew they were going to be considered as spies unless they brought Benjamin with them. We can see they had deep thoughts and agony for three days from the conversation they would have with Joseph after 3 days.

4. "If You Are Honest Men, Bring Your Youngest Brother"

Now Joseph said to them on the third day, "Do this and live, for I fear God: if you are honest men, let one of your brothers be confined in your prison; but as for the rest of you, go, carry grain for the famine of your households, and bring your youngest brother to me, so your words may be verified, and you will not die." And they did so. Then they said to one another, "Truly we are guilty concerning our brother, because we saw the distress of his soul when he pleaded with us, yet we would not listen; therefore this distress has come upon us." Reuben answered them, saying, "Did I not tell you, 'Do not sin against the boy'; and you would not listen? Now comes the reckoning for his blood." They did not know, however, that Joseph understood, for there was an interpreter between them. He turned away from them and wept. But when he returned to them and spoke to them, he took Simeon from them and bound him before their eyes. Then Joseph gave orders to fill their bags with grain and to restore every man's money in his sack, and to give them provisions for the journey. And thus it was done for them. (42:18-25)

After Joseph confined his brothers in prison for three days, he called them up and gave them a way to prove that they were not spies. He told them they were to leave one of them in prison and the rest of them could take the grain to their family, and they had to come back with their youngest brother. He told them to leave one of them behind to let them feel the pain of handing over one of their brothers to the hands of other people.

Through this, Joseph wanted to see how much love they had

among the brothers and how much they cared for each other. At the same time, it was to remind them of the fact that they had sold one of their brothers. They felt distressed at the reality that one of them had to be left behind.

As the situation reached this state, as Joseph intended, the brothers remembered their past wrongdoing and began to mention their sins amongst themselves. Of course, they couldn't even imagine the prime minister would understand their language, Hebrew, because they didn't know it was Joseph. They said, "Truly we are guilty concerning our brother, because we saw the distress of his soul when he pleaded with us, yet we would not listen; therefore this distress has come upon us."

In distress, Reuben said, "Did I not tell you, 'Do not sin against the boy'; and you would not listen? Now comes the reckoning for his blood." Because he was the firstborn he felt responsible for the fact that he couldn't stop the brothers from selling Joseph.

But he was also blaming his brothers rather than putting all the blame on himself. The brothers were regretting their fault in the past as they were put into this dire situation. They considered this situation was the retribution for their evil deed.

As Joseph was listening to the conversations among the brothers, he couldn't control his emotions. He left the scene, wept, and came back. Every situation was going as he intended. Joseph was putting his brothers into a corner in obedience to the urging of God.

But when he saw his brothers regretting their wrongdoings in the past and knowing they didn't know what to do, what might Joseph have been feeling? All the past memories flashed through his mind in an instant. He had compassion on his brothers who realized their fault and were in agony. He was sad that he couldn't reveal his identity and he had to remain strict.

He wanted to forgive his brothers immediately and hug them warmly. But he knew it was not the way that was the most beneficial for his brothers. He had to control his emotions and help them realize their sins and repent of them before God.

Selling Joseph as a slave was not just a sin against Joseph. It was also a great sin before their father Jacob and before God.

Furthermore, the brothers considered lightly the dreams that God had given to Joseph. They said to one another that they would see what would become of his dreams if they killed him (Genesis 37:20). They mocked God saying the dreams couldn't come true. They didn't just rebut the God-given dreams, but they also showed contempt for it.

The sons of Jacob had to break down these walls of sins to become the foundation stones for the nation of Israel. God couldn't form the nation of Israel through them by covering all their sins. That is why God moved Joseph's heart to let him give them a chance of repentance.

Joseph, putting aside his personal feelings, pushed his brothers into a corner. Because his brothers did not truly repent, he took

Simeon from them and bound him before their eyes. He then gave orders to fill their sacks with grain, to restore every man's money into his sack, and to give them provisions for the journey. But they didn't know the money was returned.

5. Jacob Laments Saying He Will Also Lose Benjamin

So they loaded their donkeys with their grain and departed from there. As one of them opened his sack to give his donkey fodder at the lodging place, he saw his money; and behold, it was in the mouth of his sack. Then he said to his brothers, "My money has been returned, and behold, it is even in my sack." And their hearts sank, and they turned trembling to one another, saying, "What is this that God has done to us?" When they came to their father Jacob in the land of Canaan, they told him all that had happened to them, saying, "The man, the lord of the land, spoke harshly with us, and took us for spies of the country. But we said to him, 'We are honest men; we are not spies. We are twelve brothers, sons of our father; one is no longer alive, and the youngest is with our father today in the land of Canaan.' The man, the lord of the land, said to us, 'By this I will know that you are honest men: leave one of your brothers with me and take grain for the famine of your households, and go. But bring your youngest brother to me that I may know that you are not spies, but honest men. I will give your brother to you, and you may trade in the land.' Now it came about as they were emptying their sacks, that behold, every man's bundle of money was in his sack; and when they and their father saw their bundles of money, they were dismayed." Their father Jacob said to them, "You have bereaved me of my children: Joseph is no more, and Simeon is no more, and you would take Benjamin; all these things are against me." Then Reuben spoke to his father, saying, "You may put my two sons to death if I do not bring him back to you; put him in my care, and I will return him to you." But Jacob said, "My son shall not go down with you; for his brother is dead, and he alone is left. If harm should befall him on the journey you are taking, then you will bring my gray hair down to Sheol in sorrow." (42:26-38)

Joseph's brothers stopped by a lodging place on the way back to Canaan. As one of them was opening his sack to feed his donkey, he saw the money was in the mouth of the sack. It was the money that had been brought to pay for the grain in Egypt. They became terrified because they could be accused of stealing the grain without paying for it.

As things were getting entangled even more, they couldn't help but think over why God allowed such things to happen to them. It was another chance for them to look back on their past wrongdoings.

After returning home, Joseph's brothers explained to Jacob all that had happened. They had tried to hide things before, but now they honestly explained everything; they mentioned they had to take the youngest brother, Benjamin, with them thereby exposing him to dangers; they left Simeon in Egypt; and they were now in a situation to be accused of being thieves.

It means they were ready to accept the responsibility. They were wrongfully accused and things became troublesome, but they acknowledged fundamentally that it was their fault that things had gotten out of hand.

In that situation, they could have lied to their father to avoid any further trouble. They could have said Simeon was killed by robbers and they were accused of being thieves in Egypt but barely escaped, so that they wouldn't have to go back to Egypt.

In their current situation, they couldn't be sure whether they could take Benjamin to Egypt or not. Even if they could take him there, they would be accused of being thieves. Their lives would hang in the balance. And yet, the brothers honestly explained everything to their father and tried to find a way to save Simeon.

Note that the first son, Reuben said to the father, "You may put my two sons to death if I do not bring him back to you; put him in my care, and I will return him to you." Giving the guarantee with the lives of his sons meant he had firm determination to bring Benjamin back home. His words contained true repentance for selling Joseph as a slave and breaking the heart of his father by telling him that Joseph had been killed.

Jacob was at a loss upon hearing his sons' words. He had already lost a son, and another son was captured in a foreign land. His sons said they wanted to take Benjamin to prove their innocence and bring Simeon back as well. However, Jacob knew it wouldn't be easy. Even Benjamin's life could be in danger, and he could do nothing but lament in sorrow.

What did the sons feel seeing their father in this emotional state? They had to look back on their fault in the past and repent even more deeply. This was how the brothers received the retribution for their past wrongdoing.

Even with the guarantee of Reuben, Jacob could not easily let Benjamin go. He said, if anything happened to Benjamin like in the case of Joseph, he would lose all hope of life and die. The sons couldn't do anything about their father's firm stand. There was nothing they could do apart from waiting.

Joseph
Chapter 5

Return to Egypt with Benjamin

Judah Tries to Persuade Jacob

Joseph's Brothers Took Benjamin to Egypt with Them

Brothers Became Afraid When Brought to Joseph's House

Joseph Sheds Tears of Thanksgiving

Joseph Follows the Order and Duty of Men Precisely

1. Judah Tries to Persuade Jacob

Now the famine was severe in the land. So it came about when they had finished eating the grain which they had brought from Egypt, that their father said to them, "Go back, buy us a little food." Judah spoke to him, however, saying, "The man solemnly warned us, 'You shall not see my face unless your brother is with you.' If you send our brother with us, we will go down and buy you food. But if you do not send him, we will not go down; for the man said to us, 'You will not see my face unless your brother is with you.'" Then Israel said, "Why did you treat me so badly by telling the man whether you still had another brother?" But they said, "The man questioned particularly about us and our relatives, saying, 'Is your father still alive? Have you another brother?' So we answered his questions. Could we possibly know that he would say, 'Bring your brother down'?" Judah said to his father Israel, "Send the lad with me and we will arise and go, that we may live and not die, we as well as you and our little ones. I myself will be surety for him; you may hold me responsible for him. If I do not bring him back to you and set him before you, then let me bear the blame before you forever. For if we had not delayed, surely by now we could have returned twice." (43:1-10)

The famine that hit the Near East including Egypt was catastrophic. Jacob's family couldn't avoid it either. Fortunately, they extended their lives with the food they had brought from Egypt, but it ran out quickly.

Jacob told his sons to go to Egypt to get more grain, but he did not want to allow them to take Benjamin with them. He knew they could be in danger if they didn't have Benjamin with them, and yet he was asking them to take all the risks.

Now Judah began to persuade his father saying that they had to go together with Benjamin to prove to the Egyptian prime minister that they were not spies. He said, if not, they couldn't get the grain anyway because they wouldn't be able to see the prime minister in the first place. Furthermore, the money they had paid as the price for the grain was in their sacks, and if they just went without Benjamin, they'd be considered as thieves and might be killed.

Jacob was aware of all those situations, but he wouldn't let Benjamin go easily. Not knowing what to do, he began to blame his sons, saying "Why did you treat me so badly by telling the man you still had another brother?" He put the blame on his sons. He thought they wouldn't have been in that situation if they hadn't mentioned they had yet the youngest brother at home.

Jacob couldn't see the bigger picture because of this attachment to Benjamin. He loved Benjamin very much, but the whole family could starve to death. He had to send Benjamin to Egypt so that his sons could get the grain and bring Simeon back who had been put in prison there. This was the attitude that he should have had as the head of the family.

Of course, the choice meant he had to take the risk of losing Benjamin. But neglecting the safety and lives of other family members just to protect Benjamin cannot be considered good and broad mind.

We can see Jacob's level of faith through what he did. He demolished his ego at Jabbok River and humbled himself before God, but he still had some fleshly attributes remaining in him. He still had some self-centeredness, favoritism, putting the blame on others, and serving his own interest. This keeps him from being considered completely sanctified according to the standard of sanctification in the era of the Holy Spirit.

Though their father was scolding them, the sons also had something to say. They mentioned their youngest brother because the man was asking them about their family; how could they possibly know he was going to tell them to bring him the next time they came? What they had said was true.

However, if they had tried to understand the heart of their father, they could have chosen their words more carefully. Their father lost his beloved Joseph, and the only comfort to him, Benjamin, could also be put in danger. How agonized he must have been! If they understood this heart of their father, they would have said they were sorry that they had caused such agony for their father by their indiscreet act in Egypt. Then, the situation might have been very different.

Jacob blamed his sons out of his frustration, but he knew very well that it wasn't really the fault of his sons. So, if the sons had said they were sorry, Jacob's attitude would have changed.

When there is a conflict of emotions between individuals, a word of goodness can ease the mind of the other. If they just let their tempers flare just because they feel like it, the argument and confrontation will become more serious, and they will hurt each other's feelings. Even if one person acts with evil, if the other person does not harbor any hard feelings but speaks words of goodness it can touch and ease the heart of the former, and peace will never be broken.

Also, even if both parties seem to be right in their words, their heart might not be exactly the same as their words. They might say something very reasonable, but in fact, some of them have ulterior motives.

It appears Jacob's sons were speaking for the benefit of the whole family, but that was not all there was. They were also feeling uncomfortable when their father put the blame on them and told them to go and get some more grain, without letting them take Benjamin with them. So, they argued with the desire to persuade their father to let them do what they wanted to do. Furthermore, they were hiding the fact that what they were going through was also a kind of retribution for what they had done to Joseph in the past.

Jacob and his sons were trying to find the solution within their own limits while putting the blame on each other. They should have asked God to solve the problem His way, but they were thinking only from their personal viewpoints within the given circumstances. But as the lives of all the family members were hanging in the balance, they couldn't just remain quiet about it.

So, now, Judah once again tried to persuade his father. He said that with his life he would ensure the return of Benjamin. And, if for some reason he shouldn't bring Benjamin back, he would be a sinner before Jacob forever. We can see that the situation was very urgent from his words when he said, "For if we had not delayed, surely by now we could have returned twice."

2. Joseph's Brothers Took Benjamin to Egypt with Them

Then their father Israel said to them, "If it must be so, then do this: take some of the best products of the land in your bags, and carry down to the man as a present, a little balm and a little honey, aromatic gum and myrrh, pistachio nuts and almonds. Take double the money in your hand, and take back in your hand the money that was returned in the mouth of your sacks; perhaps it was a mistake. Take your brother also, and arise, return to the man; and may God Almighty grant you compassion in the sight of the man, so that he will release to you your other brother and Benjamin. And as for me, if I am bereaved of my children, I am bereaved."

So the men took this present, and they took double the money in their hand, and Benjamin; then they arose and went down to Egypt and stood before Joseph. (43:11-15)

Jacob finally changed his mind after a series of persuasive arguments from his sons, including Judah. They all knew they didn't have a choice; the whole family would starve to death unless they quickly bought grain.

Jacob allowed them to take Benjamin with them but made a suggestion. He told them to go to Egypt with presents, the best products of the Canaan land. The present was such things as balm, honey, aromatic gum and myrrh, pistachio nuts and almonds, which were very valuable.

He also told them to take double the money for the grain. Understanding the human hearts very well, Jacob tried to ease the mind of the Egyptian prime minister and resolve any misunderstanding by giving him the presents.

It was in fact the same as the method he had used to be reconciled to his brother Esau in the past. As Proverbs 21:14 says, *"A gift in secret subdues anger,"* and such methods might prove effective, at times. But Jacob's method didn't belong to God. It wasn't a method given by God. He didn't come up with it by relying on Him and asking for His wisdom, but it was his own idea.

At the Jabbok River, decades ago, Jacob relied on God completely and experienced God's work of changing people's heart. Overnight,

God thawed the frozen heart of Esau, who had held grudges for 20 years about his birthright that had been taken away. So, Jacob should first have depended on God in the current situation, too.

But he didn't rely on God. He just let his sons prepare a present. It was an idea coming out of his own experiences. Even if we do exactly the same thing, the result will be different according to whether or not we rely on God when we do it.

Only after telling his sons to prepare the present and double the money did Jacob say, "may God Almighty grant you compassion in the sight of the man, so that he will release to you your other brother and Benjamin. And as for me, if I am bereaved of my children, I am bereaved."

Even today, when faced with a certain problem, some people use all kinds of human methods, and then, only then, do they come before God hoping for some kind of luck. Or, some others pray to God trying to commit their matters to Him, but they cannot put away using their human methods. God cannot say these people have true faith.

Those who truly leave everything to God with faith will have the assurance for the answer of God that will be given along with the peace of mind. But Jacob did everything according to his own ideas first and only then did he ask for the grace of God. Then, he said, "if I am bereaved of my children, I am bereaved," as if he was just giving up everything.

It tells us that although he was asking for God's help, he didn't have the assurance of faith or peace of mind. After all, Joseph's brothers went to Egypt and stood before Joseph bearing gifts and double the money as their father had instructed.

3. Brothers Became Afraid When Brought to Joseph's House

When Joseph saw Benjamin with them, he said to his house steward, "Bring the men into the house, and slay an animal and make ready; for the men are to dine with me at noon." So the man did as Joseph said, and brought the men to Joseph's house. Now the men were afraid, because they were brought to Joseph's house; and they said, "It is because of the money that was returned in our sacks the first time that we are being brought in, that he may seek occasion against us and fall upon us, and take us for slaves with our donkeys." So they came near to Joseph's house steward, and spoke to him at the entrance of the house, and said, "Oh, my lord, we indeed came down the first time to buy food, and it came about when we came to the lodging place, that we opened our sacks, and behold, each man's money was in the mouth of his sack, our money in full. So we have brought it back in our hand. We have also brought down other money in our hand to buy food; we do not know who put our money in our sacks." He said, "Be at ease, do not be afraid. Your God and the God of your father has given you treasure in your sacks; I had your money." Then he brought Simeon out to them. Then the man brought the men into Joseph's house and gave them water, and they washed their feet; and he gave their donkeys fodder. (43:16-24)

When Joseph saw Benjamin, who had come to Egypt with his

brothers, he told the house steward to bring his brothers into his house to dine with him. The brothers were nervous because they didn't know what was going to happen to them.

They were worried that they might be in trouble because of some misunderstanding about the money that they had paid for the grain but ended up back in their sacks. They were very afraid because they were brought to the prime minister's house without being told the reason. They thought, 'It is because of the money that was returned in our sacks the first time. They are trying to take us for slaves with our donkeys.'

As things didn't seem to be going smoothly, the brothers began to give excuses to Joseph's house steward. They said they didn't know who put the money back in their sacks, and they brought money to buy more grain in addition to the money that had been put in their sacks.

We can see the clear contrast between Joseph and his brothers. Joseph didn't give any excuse nor was he afraid even when he was put in jail due to false accusations. This is the difference in the faith they had.

When he was working in the house of the captain of the bodyguard, Joseph did not commit any sin, and for this reason he was brave even when he was wrongfully accused. He believed in God who would reveal his innocence. He believed God would guide him and depended on him completely. But his brothers couldn't either be brave or rely on God. Even excluding what they had done to Joseph, they didn't have such faith that enabled them to be bold before God.

1 John 5:18 says, *"We know that no one who is born of God sins; but He who was born of God keeps him, and the evil one does not touch him."* Those who are sinless believe that God will protect them in any situation. Even if there are tests, they still believe that they were allowed in God's love to give them blessings. But Joseph's brothers couldn't help but become afraid in disastrous or difficult situations.

Joseph's house steward said to them who were afraid, "Be at ease, do not be afraid. Your God and the God of your father has given you treasure in your sacks; I had your money."

He brought out Simeon who had been confined and gave them water so they could wash their feet. And then he gave their donkeys fodder. To their surprise, the brothers were graciously welcomed.

4. Joseph Sheds Tears of Thanksgiving

So they prepared the present for Joseph's coming at noon; for they had heard that they were to eat a meal there. When Joseph came home, they brought into the house to him the present which was in their hand and bowed to the ground before him. Then he asked them about their welfare, and said, "Is your old father well, of whom you spoke? Is he still alive?" They said, "Your servant our father is well; he is still alive." They bowed down in homage. As he lifted his eyes and saw his brother Benjamin, his mother's son, he said, "Is this your youngest brother, of whom you spoke to me?" And he said, "May God be gracious to you, my son." Joseph hurried out for he was deeply stirred over his brother, and he sought a place to weep; and he entered his chamber and wept there. Then he washed his face and came out; and he controlled himself and said, "Serve the meal." (43:25-31)

The brothers were informed that they were going to dine with the prime minister of Egypt. When Joseph came to the house at noon, they gave the presents to him and bowed down in homage. They wanted to find favor in his eyes by humbling themselves exceedingly.

Now Joseph first asked about their father Jacob saying, "Is your old father well, of whom you spoke? Is he still alive?" He knew his father was alive the last time, but he wanted to ask about his welfare again because it had been a while since then.

Joseph must have missed his father very much because it had already been more than 20 years since he was parted from his father who loved him very much. And yet, Joseph controlled himself not to reveal his identity and continued to obey God's urging. Of course it is human duty to love and serve their family members, but sometimes one has to follow the guidance of God with regard to family, by cutting off passion and fleshly affection toward them (1 Timothy 5:8; Galatians 5:24).

As Joseph asked about their father, the brothers replied, "Your servant our father is well; he is still alive."

After asking about his father, Joseph looked for his younger brother Benjamin. It had taken 13 years from the time he was sold as a slave into Egypt until he became the prime minister. And there used to be seven years of abundance, and now it was the second year of the famine (Genesis 45:6). So, he saw his brother Benjamin in 22 years.

On meeting Benjamin, what kinds of emotions do you think Joseph had? Benjamin was a little boy when they were parted, and now he was a grown man. Since Benjamin had lost his mother at birth, Joseph must have felt sorry that he couldn't have been with Benjamin as he grew up.

Joseph said to Benjamin, "May God be gracious to you, my son." He wanted just a little bit of his affection to be delivered to him. If the brothers were spiritually sensitive, they wouldn't have missed these words. It was certainly an unusual thing for the Egyptian prime minister to say.

When Joseph's brothers first met him, he said, "I fear God." He gave a clue to his brothers so they could realize what they were supposed to do. But they just missed it too. Why?

They wondered how to get out of the situation at the time and their minds were full of fleshly thoughts in agony. So, rather than catching the clue from Joseph's words, they were afraid of what he was going to say next. They weren't spiritually awakened because of their fleshly thoughts.

With your mind focused elsewhere, you wouldn't grasp the answer even if the answer is given into your hand. Even if others give you a clue or directly point out something to you, you wouldn't understand their point when your mind is filled with your own thoughts.

Those who are drenched in fleshly thoughts cannot gain spiritual understanding. They might even pass judgment and condemnation on others for what they hear. Therefore, we should remember fleshly thoughts are such great obstacles to understanding God's will.

Shortly after he gave warm words to Benjamin, Joseph's emotions which had been suppressed burst out at last. He couldn't control himself any more. He sought a place to weep and entered his chamber. Endless tears ran down on his face. They were tears of thanksgiving as well as happiness at having met his younger brother.

He was thankful that his brother grew up well even though he couldn't be there for him and that they were able to meet again. Joseph looked at every situation with the eyes of thanksgiving. He offered up aroma of thanksgiving not only when things were good but also in every moment. He understood the good will of God in each situation.

5. Joseph Follows the Order and Duty of Men Precisely

So they served him by himself, and them by themselves, and the Egyptians who ate with him by themselves, because the Egyptians could not eat bread with the Hebrews, for that is loathsome to the Egyptians. Now they were seated before him, the firstborn according to his birthright and the youngest according to his youth, and the men looked at one another in astonishment. He took portions to them from his own table, but Benjamin's portion was five times as much as any of theirs. So they feasted and drank freely with him. (43:32-34)

Joseph washed his face and controlled himself before he came out to his brothers and dined with them. People served Joseph by himself, and his brothers by themselves, and the Egyptians who ate with him by themselves, because Egyptians considered it loathsome to eat bread with Hebrews.

Just by seeing this scene we can understand what kind of heart and attitude Joseph had to pursue peace. What does this mean?

Egyptians knew very well Joseph was a Hebrew. Even though he was the second most powerful man in Egypt only next to the king, Egyptians wouldn't want to eat with him, since he was still a Hebrew. If Joseph had possessed ill feelings against them and tried to reign over them as the prime minister, there would have been some conflicts between him and them.

But Joseph didn't try to force them to act against their customs or ignore them just because he had the power. He respected their customs and religion. And yet, as a believer in God, he would never compromise with their religion or do anything that could disappoint God.

He always gave glory to God and showed the existence of God through his life. For this reason, the Egyptians acknowledged the God that Joseph believed in, and trusted his words.

What if Joseph's duty was that of a prophet, to proclaim the living God in Egypt? He'd have boldly proclaimed God without any reservation or fear. He wouldn't have hesitated at all even in a situation when he had to stand up against Egypt's customs or religion.

But his duty was not to proclaim the living God in Egypt, and he pursued peace with everybody. The Egyptians were also aware that Joseph understood them with his good and broad heart, so they didn't have to keep him in check or dislike him. They respected and served him with their hearts.

Joseph sat the brothers exactly in the order of birth. The brothers were obviously very surprised because they didn't know who the prime minister was. But nothing beyond that was came upon them. They just wondered how the prime minister had found out the order among the brothers.

Why did then Joseph sit them in the exact order of birth? It was to serve them in accordance with the order and duty of men. He didn't favor Benjamin just because he was born of the same mother, nor did he put those brothers who had a better relationship with him closer to him. He did this with the heart of service to his brothers because he didn't have any hard feelings against them. He showed hospitality by giving them portions of food from his own table.

The brothers' minds were put at ease. They joyfully accepted his hospitality and enjoyed the meal. Joseph gave five times more food to Benjamin than to other brothers. Why did he do so?

Joseph couldn't help it. As an older brother he hadn't done anything for Benjamin for more than 20 years. He was sorry that Benjamin had to be on his own among his half-brothers all those years.

Joseph wanted to make it up to Benjamin for those times. He expressed this kind of emotion by giving five times more portion to Benjamin than to other brothers. He could have given three times more or four times more, but the reason why he gave five times more is because he felt it was enough. It means he was not drawn by fleshly affection but acted according to the urging of God.

Herein lies an important spiritual meaning: God pays us back according to our deeds. Benjamin was the only one among the brothers who didn't participate in selling Joseph as a slave. Of course, he was too young to be present at the scene. But even if he had been there with them, he would never have partaken in selling his own brother.

God blessed Benjamin in a special way because he was the only one who didn't partake in the evil of selling his brother. Therefore, we should understand how important it is not to partake in evil or create a wall of sin before God.

Add-in 3

Levels of Forgiveness

Dictionary definition of 'forgive' is "to give up resentment against or stop wanting to punish (someone) for an offense or fault." The biblical meaning of forgiveness is to be able to forgive even those who can't be forgiven as well as those who can be forgiven.

Peter once asked Jesus, *"Lord, how often shall my brother sin against me and I forgive him? Up to seven times?"* (Matthew 18:21) People mostly have limits in their forgiveness. But God's forgiveness is different. Jesus replied, *"I do not say to you, up to seven times, but up to seventy times seven"* (Matthew 18:22). 'Seven' is the number of perfection, and 'to forgive seventy times seven' means 'to forgive limitlessly and completely.'

The completeness of forgiveness is different from person to person, too. Some say they have forgiven but have remaining resentment within them. But God forgives even those who can't be forgiven, and He does not remember it at all. God's love does not end at forgiving. In fact forgiving is just the beginning. He gives deeper love beginning with forgiveness.

1. Reluctant Forgiveness

You don't really want to forgive, and you still have resentment, but you can pretend to be forgiving. If the other person is higher in the rank or if you need to get some help from them, you may say you forgive them, but it's only for your benefit. So, if the other person is lower in the rank or they have nothing to do with your personal gain, your attitude will be different. You will think you don't have to suppress your feelings, and you easily express your emotions outwardly in words and action. Reluctant forgiveness is not true forgiveness; but it is rather more of hypocrisy.

2. Forgiveness to Follow God's Word

You don't completely forgive the other person even though you try to forgive them because you know you have to forgive them according to the Word of God. In this case, you can forgive only within your limits because you haven't completely cultivated goodness in your heart. When the situation goes over your limit, you will reveal your ill-feelings. But as you keep on trying to practice the truth, the Word of God, you can reach the level where you can forgive them from heart.

3. Forgiveness from Heart

Even though the other person has caused great damage to you, you don't raise a question about it. You have forgiven with compassion and without any hard feelings. But if they shamelessly ask you for more help, you think they are over the line. You think you have shown enough mercy by forgiving them, so you cannot give them any more than that.

4. Beyond Forgiveness with Limitless Mercy

Colossians 3:13-14 says, *"... bearing with one another, and forgiving each other, whoever has a complaint against anyone; just as the Lord forgave you, so also should you. Beyond all these things put on love, which is the perfect bond of unity."* Even after forgiving somebody for something that can't be forgiven, you will still care for them. Even if they ask for more help, you will give to them again and again unless the Holy Spirit stops you. And yet, you do not have any uncomfortable feelings. You just sincerely desire that they will demolish their walls of sin, so that they will be forgiven and be acknowledged by God again.

If we think about the grace and love we have received from God, there is nobody whom we cannot forgive. However, unconditional forgiveness is not always an act of goodness. If the others do not try to change themselves at all even though they were forgiven many times, it means they are building up more walls of sin against God. In this kind of case, rather than forgiving them unconditionally, you should wait for them to be forgiven through their true repentance.

Joseph

Chapter 6

Joseph Changes His Brothers with Wisdom of Goodness

"Put My Silver Cup and His Money for the Grain Back in His Sack"

Joseph Tests Love among His Brothers

Judah Earnestly Pleads to Save Benjamin

1. "Put My Silver Cup and His Money for the Grain in His Sack"

Then he commanded his house steward, saying, "Fill the men's sacks with food, as much as they can carry, and put each man's money in the mouth of his sack. Put my cup, the silver cup, in the mouth of the sack of the youngest, and his money for the grain." And he did as Joseph had told him. As soon as it was light, the men were sent away, they with their donkeys. They had just gone out of the city, and were not far off, when Joseph said to his house steward, "Up, follow the men; and when you overtake them, say to them, 'Why have you repaid evil for good? Is not this the one from which my lord drinks and which he indeed uses for divination? You have done wrong in doing this.' So he overtook them and spoke these words to them. They said to him, "Why does my lord speak such words as these? Far be it from your servants to do such a thing. Behold, the money which we found in the mouth of our sacks we have brought back to you from the land of Canaan. How then could we steal silver or gold from your lord's house? With whomever of your servants it is found, let him die, and we also will be my lord's slaves." So he said, "Now let it also be according to your words; he with whom it is found shall be my slave, and the rest of you shall be innocent." Then they hurried, each man lowered his sack to the ground, and each man opened his sack. He searched, beginning with the oldest and ending with the youngest, and the cup was found in Benjamin's sack. Then they tore their clothes, and when each man loaded his donkey, they returned to the city. (44:1-13)

After serving his brothers with warm hospitality, he commanded his house steward to fill their sacks with grain. Also, Joseph had him secretly put each one's money back in their sacks and hide his silver cup in Benjamin's sack. Without knowing this fact, the brothers headed back home with joyful minds.

Unlike their worries, they were not harmed in anyway, and Simeon who had been confined was also with them now. But their joy didn't last long. They were not far off from the city when Joseph's house steward hastily caught up with them and said, "Why have you repaid evil for good?" And he said something they couldn't understand at all. It was that they had stolen something from the house of the prime minister.

Being accused of being thieves, the brothers were dumb-founded. They argued their innocence saying they brought back the money that had been in their sacks, and they couldn't possibly steal from the prime minister of Egypt. They also said with whomever the cup was found, he would die, and they also would be the slaves of the prime minister.

They put the sacks down on the ground without any hesitation and searched them beginning from the first son. But to their astonishment, the silver cup was found in Benjamin's sack. The brothers were all shocked and turned ghastly pale.

Their father hated the idea of sending Benjamin with them, and Judah persuaded him to let him come with them by putting his own life as collateral. But now the situation turned in such a way that Benjamin couldn't go back home. With this clear evidence, the brothers had to go back to the prime minister's house.

2. Joseph Tests Love among His Brothers

When Judah and his brothers came to Joseph's house, he was still there, and they fell to the ground before him. Joseph said to them, "What is this deed that you have done? Do you not know that such a man as I can indeed practice divination?" So Judah said, "What can we say to my lord? What can we speak? And how can we justify ourselves? God has found out the iniquity of your servants; behold, we are my lord's slaves, both we and the one in whose possession the cup has been found." But he said, "Far be it from me to do this. The man in whose possession the cup has been found, he shall be my slave; but as for you, go up in peace to your father." (44:14-17)

Joseph was already waiting for them at his house. The brothers fell to the ground before him, although they were wrongfully accused. But pretending to know nothing about their innocence,

Joseph said to them with a stern voice, "What is this deed that you have done?"

Because the silver cup was found in Benjamin's sack, the brothers didn't stand a chance. But thinking of the father who was waiting for them back home along with Benjamin, they were desperate to save Benjamin.

Judah stood up and said, "What can we say to my lord? What can we speak? And how can we justify ourselves? God has found out the iniquity of your servants; behold, we are my lord's slaves, both we and the one in whose possession the cup has been found." He felt very troubled because there was no way for them to prove their innocence, and he said that God had found out their iniquity.

The brothers remembered the time when they sold Joseph to the traders. Even though he begged them, they just ignored him and sold him. But as they were wrongfully accused now, they came to feel similar kind of emotion that Joseph had when he was being sold. Also, they could imprint on their mind that one receives retribution according to his deeds.

Even though they came to gain this realization and regretted the past, it didn't mean they could change the current situation. They were in a situation to become the slaves of the Egyptian prime minister as Judah said.

But the Egyptian prime minister says only Benjamin, in whose possession the silver cup was found, would be his slave and the rest could go back home. Now, what do you think the brothers' reaction was?

In reality, they couldn't keep their promise to their father to bring back Benjamin. In their former manner of life, they would have thought the situation turned out fine. They could have said all the brothers could have become slaves but fortunately only Benjamin would be one. They would have tried to tell their father a lie and convince him something unexpected had happened to Benjamin. But now, the attitudes of the brothers were different.

3. Judah Earnestly Pleads to Save Benjamin

Then Judah approached him, and said, "Oh my lord, may your servant please speak a word in my lord's ears, and do not be angry with your servant; for you are equal to Pharaoh. My lord asked his servants, saying, 'Have you a father or a brother?' We said to my lord, 'We have an old father and a little child of his old age. Now his brother is dead, so he alone is left of his mother, and his father loves him.' Then you said to your servants, 'Bring him down to me that I may set my eyes on him.' But we said to my lord, 'The lad cannot leave his father, for if he should leave his father, his father would die.' You said to your servants, however, 'Unless your youngest brother comes down with you, you will not see my face again.' Thus it came about when we went up to your servant my father, we told him the words of my lord. Our father said, 'Go back, buy us a little food.' But we said, 'We cannot go down. If our youngest brother is with us, then we will go down; for we cannot see the man's face unless our youngest brother is with us.' Your servant my father said to us, 'You know that my wife bore me two sons; and the one went out from me, and I said, "Surely he is torn in pieces," and I have not seen him since. If you take this one also from me, and harm befalls him, you will bring my gray hair down to Sheol in sorrow.' Now, therefore, when I come to your servant my father, and the lad is not with us, since his life is bound up in the lad's life, when he sees that the lad is not with us, he will die. Thus your servants will bring the gray hair of your servant our father down to Sheol in sorrow. For your servant became surety for the lad to my father, saying, 'If I do not bring him back to you, then let me bear the blame before my father forever.' Now, therefore, please let your servant remain instead of the lad a slave to my lord, and let the lad go up with his brothers. For how shall I go up to my father if the lad is not with me for fear that I see the evil that would overtake my father?" (44:18-34)

In the eyes of the brothers Joseph was the same as Pharaoh. It seemed that he had absolute power because he was doing his job as the prime minister with all Pharaoh's authorities bestowed on him. Judah approached this Joseph and began to explain everything respectfully.

He reminded Joseph of the fact that they were accused of being spies and that Joseph told them to bring their youngest brother to Egypt in order to prove they were not spies. He also explained it wasn't easy at all to bring him because their father cherished Benjamin as his own life.

He added if they couldn't bring Benjamin back to their

home country their old father would be in such deep sorrow and eventually die of sadness. He suggested he would remain as a slave and implored to send Benjamin back home. His words contained concerns for Benjamin, his determination to keep his promise with his father, and his heartfelt concern for his father about the pain he would have to suffer in case he couldn't keep his promise.

Through these words we can see that he and other brothers were no longer the same as before. They were different from the time when they had sold Joseph as a slave and cheated their father with lies. It was painful for them to go back home leaving Simeon behind, and now they couldn't possibly go back leaving Benjamin behind.

They had no intention to cheat their father or just to let themselves live at the cost of sacrificing one of the brothers. Judah knew what kind of life he'd have to live if he remained there as a slave, and yet, he volunteered to be left behind in place of Benjamin.

This was how Joseph, through wisdom given from above, led his brothers to realize their fault of the past from the heart and repent of it. This was the way of love for them.

What if they didn't go through such things? They wouldn't have realized their sin for the rest of their lives. For the moment they had to suffer some pain but they came to repent before God and Joseph through such moments, and thus, the momentary suffering turned into blessing for them.

In the past, they were jealous of each other. They only thought in their own viewpoints. Of course, Joseph also acted in a way that would have given rise to hatred of the brothers by bringing bad reports about his brothers to his father. But that doesn't mean the brothers were justified in trying to kill him and selling him off as a slave. Their hearts were evil in that sense. Furthermore, they knew their father would be tormented and yet they lied to him saying Joseph was torn by a beast. Then they covered it up for more than 20 years.

Of course, some of them had some pangs of conscience, but they wouldn't willingly confess their sins and repent until God allowed them trials. It was difficult to expect true love among the brothers from them or heart-felt respect and service to their father.

What if they had formed the nation of Israel without going through the trial to reveal their faults? They would never be united, being jealous of each other and trying to keep each other in check. When faced with difficulties, they'd only serve their own interests rather than sacrificing themselves and yielding to others.

But now, they yield and sacrifice themselves for each other. Even if just one of them receives love and blessings, they don't complain about it. They just understand each other and pursue peace. They now respect and honor their father Jacob from their heart and obey him.

If Joseph had revealed his identity from the beginning and acted according to his fleshly affections, such changes wouldn't have taken place. But he obeyed God's guidance with self-control and endurance and led his brothers to repentance.

Joseph was so happy to see his brothers acknowledging their

faults thoroughly and repenting from the heart. Especially, seeing they were willing to sacrifice themselves for Benjamin, his emotions that he had suppressed erupted instantly. He felt that it was the moment when he could reveal his identity and enjoy the joy of meeting his brothers to the fullest.

God's work always has the right time, and if we obey God's guidance, we will certainly harvest good fruit. But generally, people put their own benefits and their emotions ahead of God's guidance. They can't wait for the right moment, and many things go wrong.

Through Joseph's case, we can understand the importance of waiting for the right time and following the guidance of God. But this right time has to be in accordance with the justice. Namely, if the repentance of the brothers was not enough, or if they didn't repent in truth and in heart, God wouldn't have urged Joseph's heart the way He did.

Therefore, the right time is also up to the people in this sense. If the brothers didn't repent but only thought about their own well-being, the right time would have been put off. On the contrary, if they repented enough to please God when they came to Egypt the first time, the right time would have been sooner.

Joseph

Chapter 7

"You Must Hurry and Bring My Father Down Here"

"Do Not Be Grieved Because You Sold Me Here"

"God Has Made Me Lord of All Egypt"

"Take Your Father and Your Households and Come to Me"

"I will Go and See Him before I Die"

1. "Do Not Be Grieved Because You Sold Me Here"

Then Joseph could not control himself before all those who stood by him, and he cried, "Have everyone go out from me." So there was no man with him when Joseph made himself known to his brothers. He wept so loudly that the Egyptians heard it, and the household of Pharaoh heard of it. Then Joseph said to his brothers, "I am Joseph! Is my father still alive?" But his brothers could not answer him, for they were dismayed at his presence. Then Joseph said to his brothers, "Please come closer to me." And they came closer. And he said, "I am your brother Joseph, whom you sold into Egypt. Now do not be grieved or angry with yourselves, because you sold me here, for God sent me before you to preserve life." (45:1-5)

Joseph couldn't control himself any longer and had everyone around leave him. He revealed his identity to his brothers and wept loudly. As he finally revealed his identity before his brothers, all the memories came back to him. It doesn't mean he was angry at his brothers for causing him all his past hardships. He was thankful for God's guidance until that moment. Thinking of the love and blessings of God who guided him with delicate hands until that moment, his tears didn't stop running down on his face.

He had missed his father and brothers, and he missed Benjamin most especially with deep love. When all these emotions came up, he couldn't control himself. He had had to suppress these feelings although he missed his family and wanted to be with them so much. But now he didn't have to do that any longer. His affection and deep emotions were so great that it caused him to weep so loudly that it was heard by the Egyptians and even to the palace of the Pharaoh.

Joseph had everyone around him leave him before he revealed himself before his brothers. We can see his broad-mindedness here as well. The relationship between Joseph and his servants was not just a master-servant relationship. Joseph always cared for his subordinates and even served them from his heart. He never put any pressure on them or gave them a hard time. Thus, the servants also served him with all their heart and tried to do the things in a way that was pleasing to him.

And what if Joseph had wept so loudly before all his servants being unable to control himself? All the servants would have felt very embarrassed as they were watching him weep so loudly. They wouldn't have known what to do at all. That is why before he could share the joy of meeting with his brothers again, Joseph had them go out and away from him so as not to put them in such an embarrassing situation. Even in such a moment he was considering the standpoint of his subordinates.

Another reason why Joseph had all his people leave him was

because of his brothers, too. How shocking would it have been for the brothers when they found out the prime minister of Egypt was Joseph? They couldn't possibly imagine they were standing right in front of him, because they thought Joseph was living as a slave if he wasn't dead.

The brothers were in a dilemma because they couldn't treat Joseph as either the prime minister of Egypt or their younger brother. If the servants had watched all these things, the brothers would have found it more difficult to say anything to Joseph. How could they say anything freely as they were shocked and the servants were watching them attentively?

Considering this kind of standpoint of his brothers, Joseph had his people leave him. He wanted his brothers to be in the most comfortable situation possible as they were going to share the joy of meeting again.

Joseph then asked his brothers about his father. But the brothers were so astonished that they couldn't answer. They had so many different kinds of thoughts flashing through their minds.

In fact, until Joseph revealed his identity, they were in a dire situation. So, as they came to know that the prime minister who had the authority over their lives was their brother Joseph, they were relieved. They had the hope that the situation could be resolved dramatically.

But soon, they remembered what they had done to Joseph and became nervous again. They were afraid that Joseph might want to pay them back for what they had done to him.

Understanding this concern of the brothers, Joseph tried to put their minds at ease. He asked them to come closer and said, "I am your brother Joseph, whom you sold into Egypt. Now do not be grieved or angry with yourselves, because you sold me here."

Joseph didn't say "...whom you sold into Egypt..." with anger or resentment. He said it to bring back the memory of his brothers who were not able to recognize him right away.

After soothing his brothers' minds, he stated the providence of God contained in what had happened. He said, "God sent me before you to preserve life." What an emotional statement! It was a kind of word that could come out of extremely good heartedness that had no evil at all.

If we try to look for the will of God with a thankful heart, we will see the plan and will of God, and we will be even more thankful. For us to be able to do so, above all, we must not have evil in our heart.

If Joseph hadn't wanted to forgive his brothers, he wouldn't have been able to see the good will of God or the reason why God had sent him to Egypt and made him the prime minister.

But he had already forgiven his brothers and relied on God alone. He always believed God would lead his life. For this reason he could realize the good will of God and he was now able to explain it to his brothers. He did not just comfort them saying they wouldn't be worried, but encouraged them saying that blessed moment had come through the things in the past. It was beyond the level of forgiveness, and active goodness that could move others' heart.

An ordinary person would have wanted revenge and tried to

seek vengeance against his brothers. Or, he could have pretended he had forgiven them but actually he could look down on them taking pride in his success. But it was not the case with Joseph. He forgave his brothers from the heart, and furthermore, he had the goodness in heart even to comfort them and touch their hearts. That is why God chose him to fulfill His providence.

2. "God Has Made Me Lord of All Egypt"

"For the famine has been in the land these two years, and there are still five years in which there will be neither plowing nor harvesting. God sent me before you to preserve for you a remnant in the earth, and to keep you alive by a great deliverance. Now, therefore, it was not you who sent me here, but God; and He has made me a father to Pharaoh and lord of all his household and ruler over all the land of Egypt. Hurry and go up to my father, and say to him, 'Thus says your son Joseph, "God has made me lord of all Egypt; come down to me, do not delay. You shall live in the land of Goshen, and you shall be near me, you and your children and your children's children and your flocks and your herds and all that you have. There I will also provide for you, for there are still five years of famine to come, and you and your household and all that you have would be impoverished."' Behold, your eyes see, and the eyes of my brother Benjamin see, that it is my mouth which is speaking to you. Now you must tell my father of all my splendor in Egypt, and all that you have seen; and you must hurry and bring my father down here." Then he fell on his brother Benjamin's neck and wept, and Benjamin wept on his neck.

He kissed all his brothers and wept on them, and afterward his brothers talked with him. (45:6-15)

His brothers were at a loss, and to them Joseph continued to explain God's providence in more detail. In Egypt, the seven years of abundance passed and they were having the second year of famine at the moment. There still remained five years of severe famine. In neighboring countries food was already scarce, and they had to come to Egypt to buy grain. Jacob's family was no exception.

The famine would last for five more years and it would have been very difficult for them to survive in their homeland. Even if they could, it wasn't going to be easy to get their wealth back in the barren land. Foreknowing everything, God sent Joseph to Egypt first to prepare a way for the whole family to be saved.

God's providence was to establish Jacob as the father of Israel and form the nation of Israel through his twelve sons. And to fulfill this providence, God prepared a way with His amazing wisdom beyond the grasp of men. It was to send Joseph to Egypt first and make him the prime minister.

But it wasn't something easy at all to make him the prime minister of Egypt in such a short time. It was a virtual impossibility. And God would never just make Joseph the prime minister against all the rules and order of the nature. So, He worked in the quickest way possible, and Joseph believed in the good will of God and overcame everything with a thankful heart. After he became the prime minister, Joseph more clearly understood God's will and His plan for him.

Joseph explained the providence of God in detail to his brothers and delivered God's love to them. He said, "God sent me before you to preserve for you a remnant in the earth, and to keep you alive by a great deliverance. Now, therefore, it was not you who sent me here, but God; and He has made me a father to Pharaoh and lord of all his household and ruler over all the land of Egypt."

It means God sent him to Egypt in advance and put him at a very high position to save his father Jacob and the family from the severe famine. In order to form a nation through Jacob's family, they had to overcome various threats from the many peoples around them, and for this reason God put them under the protection of the strong Egypt. God prepared the most suitable environment for the future of Israel, which was like a fence that could protect them until they could pass through the famine and become a big nation.

Those who truly revere God and rely on Him will try to understand God's will and providence in any kind of trial, and they will wait quietly until God's will is revealed. Then, eventually, God's plan will be fulfilled and they will give glory to God.

Joseph believed in God's will and plan. He waited silently with a grateful heart during his trials. Finally, he was able to reveal the glory of God. What is important here is that when one gains honor like Joseph, he has to give all the glory to God alone.

If he tries to reveal himself or enjoy being honored, he can't be used perfectly by God, and even if he is used by God for a moment, he will be forsaken. Therefore, we must never think that it is we who accomplished something (1 Corinthians 10:12). We should always bear in mind that we are only instruments for God's glory, and never deviate from it.

Joseph was well aware that he didn't become the prime minister because of his intelligence or for him to gain honor. He didn't try to earn the approval of others. He only wanted to reveal the glory of God and to be an instrument in fulfilling His providence. Also, when he invited his father and family to Egypt, it wasn't out of his personal compassion or for his personal gain.

Of course, he wanted to share the blessings that God had given him with the rest of his family members. But it wasn't only for his family. It was to fulfill God's providence to form a nation based on that blessing. In this way, when a person shows goodness to others and shares blessings with them, one might do it out of his own desires and greed while another might do it following the will of God.

In order to fully accomplish the providence of God, Joseph urged his brothers to go back to his father, Jacob, quickly and deliver the news about him. He wanted them to tell Jacob that God appointed him as the prime minister of Egypt and tell him about everything they'd seen and heard in Egypt. There remained five more years of famine ahead of them, so he wanted to put his father and the family near him and take care of them.

After saying all these things to his brothers, Joseph finally embraced Benjamin and wept. The tears were running down out of deep love and longing for him. He also kissed his brothers and embraced them and wept. He didn't have any personal feelings because he'd forgiven them from the bottom of his heart. Instead, he accepted and loved them very much. How shocked and touched his brothers must have been! They repented of their past evil once again. They were happy being filled with thankfulness toward Joseph.

3. "Take Your Father and Your Households and Come to Me"

Now when the news was heard in Pharaoh's house that Joseph's brothers had come, it pleased Pharaoh and his servants. Then Pharaoh said to Joseph, "Say to your brothers, 'Do this: load your beasts and go to the land of Canaan, and take your father and your households and come to me, and I will give you the best of the land of Egypt and you will eat the fat of the land.' Now you are ordered, 'Do this: take wagons from the land of Egypt for your little ones and for your wives, and bring your father and come. Do not concern yourselves with your goods, for the best of all the land of Egypt is yours.'" (45:16-20)

The news about Joseph's brothers being in Egypt was spread to Pharaoh's palace as well. Pharaoh and his servants were very happy to hear this news. It proves Joseph had complete trust and love of Pharaoh as well as his servants.

Pharaoh happily told Joseph to bring his family to Egypt. He also said he would give them the best of the land of Egypt. He gave the wagons for Joseph's father, the little ones, and the women and said, "Do not concern yourselves with your goods"

Here, "goods" refers to all the utensils, tools, machines, and everything that was in the household. So, "Do not concern yourselves with your goods" means there are more than enough goods in Egypt, and they didn't have to bring them all the way from Canaan. Pharaoh was showing the greatest hospitality he could.

To Pharaoh, Joseph was the savior who saved Egypt. If it weren't for Joseph, Egypt would have had to suffer terribly from the famine. Joseph was literally a blessing to Pharaoh, and Pharaoh wanted to pay back this grace by showing hospitality to his family.

Also, Pharaoh thought that if Joseph's family came to Egypt, he would be comforted and strengthened so that he could focus on the administration of the country even more completely. In addition, he thought Joseph's brothers would also be intelligent and capable individuals and they could make contributions to the country, for they were the family of Joseph who had wisdom from heaven.

The reason why Joseph received complete love and trust from Pharaoh was not just because he helped the nation of Egypt very much. It was also because his behaviors and attitudes were more than enough to be acknowledged. He did not misuse his authority and power just because he was the highest ranking person next only to Pharaoh.

He never stepped out of line. He didn't have any ulterior motives or greed, so he let everything that belonged to Pharaoh return to Pharaoh. He never made any mistakes, and he always produced greater results than Pharaoh expected. That is why Egypt was stable and had peace even during the severe famine. In fact, Egypt was not just at peace, but it became even richer and stronger and the power of its ruler was solidified.

For all these reasons, Pharaoh could entrust everything to Joseph having complete trust in him. Pharaoh's servants also respected and trusted Joseph. Joseph never looked down on them or acted unbecomingly toward them. He was always respectful considering others first.

Even if he could see some faults in people, he covered them over and accepted them. He accepted even those who stood against him. He had the heart that was broad enough to pursue peace with everyone. This was how he could earn the heart of Pharaoh's servants, too.

In this situation, when the news was delivered that Joseph's brothers came, the ministers also rejoiced together. After all, it was Joseph's humility that led him to the noble position (Proverbs 18:12), and his wisdom of goodness was the key to gaining the hearts of the people in a foreign country.

4. "I will Go and See Him before I Die"

Then the sons of Israel did so; and Joseph gave them wagons according to the command of Pharaoh, and gave them provisions for the journey. To each of them he gave changes of garments, but to Benjamin he gave three hundred pieces of silver and five changes of garments. To his father he sent as follows: ten donkeys loaded with the best things of Egypt, and ten female donkeys loaded with grain and bread and sustenance for his father on the journey. So he sent his brothers away, and as they departed, he said to them, "Do not quarrel on the journey." Then they went up from Egypt, and came to the land of Canaan to their father Jacob. They told him, saying, "Joseph is still alive, and indeed he is ruler over all the land of Egypt." But he was stunned, for he did not believe them. When they told him all the words of Joseph that he had spoken to them, and when he saw the wagons that Joseph had sent to carry him, the spirit of their father Jacob revived. Then Israel said, "It is enough; my son Joseph is still alive. I will go and see him before I die." (45:21-28)

Joseph gave them wagons according to the command of Pharaoh, and gave them provisions for the journey and many precious gifts. The reason for giving them many gifts was to convince his father to leave his home country and come down to Egypt.

Canaan was the land that God had promised to give to Abraham, Isaac, and Jacob. Thus, it wasn't something easy for Jacob to decide to leave that land and move to Egypt. Joseph understood very well what kind of meaning the land had to his father. For this reason he sent many gifts through his brothers to convince him that he really was the prime minister in Egypt and that everything was in the providence of God.

Here, Joseph once again gave more gifts to his younger brother Benjamin than to his other brothers. The other brothers wouldn't be jealous of something like this now. They were changed through trials.

Lastly, he advised his brothers not to quarrel on the journey. It was a preemptive measure to bear the fruit completely. What does this mean? God had refined Joseph to establish him as the prime minister of Egypt and He also disciplined Joseph's brothers to transform them. It was all in the providence of God to make Israel a great nation.

Now, when Jacob and his households came to Egypt and settled there, it was going to be the beginning point of bearing the fruit of God's providence for Israel. But, what if the brothers would quarrel with each other on the journey and the peace be broken at this crucial moment? It means it would have given Satan grounds for accusations against them and the fulfillment of God's providence might have been postponed.

Joseph's brothers were changed, but it didn't mean they had cultivated complete goodness. Thus, there was a chance that the untruthful attributes remaining in their hearts could come up on the journey back home. Perhaps they could have quarreled about which one did more work, or they could complain about the distribution of the gifts with their greed for material things. Maybe, while they were talking about the past, they could have put the blame on each other and argued.

If such a thing had happened, it would have given Satan grounds for accusations just before the fulfillment of God's plan. Joseph gave advice to his brothers because he was well aware of this law of the spiritual realm.

Finally, the brothers arrived home. They explained to their father, Jacob, everything that had happened. They said Joseph was alive and he was the prime minister of Egypt. Jacob couldn't believe them. For 22 years he had thought Joseph was torn by a beast after seeing his varicolored tunic. Now he couldn't believe a word they were saying.

But because Joseph anticipated such a situation, he told his brothers what to tell their father in detail. He advised them to tell him everything they had seen with their eyes in Egypt. Additionally he sent ten donkeys loaded with the best things of Egypt and ten female donkeys loaded with grain and bread and sustenance for his father on the journey.

Jacob finally believed their words after hearing all the words Joseph had delivered to him and seeing all the wagons and gifts. How overwhelmed he must have been hearing that his beloved son was alive and had become the prime minister of Egypt and that he sent the wagons and bread and was waiting for him! Jacob's heart was filled with yearning for him and overjoyed with the fact that Joseph was alive.

I believe all the things that will take place from now
Will be in accordance with
God's providence and will.
Let God's grace overflow in this place.
And let His grace not stop through God's people.

I give thanks.
I give thanks for loving me.
I give thanks for giving me grace.
I give thanks for letting me be in all of this glory.
I also give thanks for letting me close my eyes in this glory.

I commit everything to God.
I go to Your bosom in peace.
Embrace me, Your son, Your pleasing son,
in Your bosom, Father,
And be glad.

Part 3

Joseph, Passageway of God's Covenant

Part 3

Joseph's life journey was a process and passageway in which God's covenant with Abraham, Isaac, and Jacob was being fulfilled.

He laid the foundation for the formation of the nation of Israel because he believed in the good will of God. He also fulfilled God's providence to save the lives of all peoples.

Joseph

Chapter 8

Jacob's Family in Goshen

"I Will Make You a Great Nation There"

Jacob's Household Moved to Egypt

When Pharaoh Calls You and Says, 'What is Your Occupation?'

1. "I Will Make You a Great Nation There"

So Israel set out with all that he had, and came to Beersheba, and offered sacrifices to the God of his father Isaac. God spoke to Israel in visions of the night and said, "Jacob, Jacob." And he said, "Here I am." He said, "I am God, the God of your father; do not be afraid to go down to Egypt, for I will make you a great nation there. I will go down with you to Egypt, and I will also surely bring you up again; and Joseph will close your eyes." Then Jacob arose from Beersheba; and the sons of Israel carried their father Jacob and their little ones and their wives in the wagons which Pharaoh had sent to carry him. They took their livestock and their property, which they had acquired in the land of Canaan, and came to Egypt, Jacob and all his descendants with him: his sons and his grandsons with him, his daughters and his granddaughters, and all his descendants he brought with him to Egypt. (46:1-7)

Now, all Jacob had to do was just get on the wagon sent by Pharaoh and go down to Egypt where Joseph was waiting. But he couldn't immediately leave. It's because of the special meaning that the Canaan land carried. Canaan was the Promised Land that God had given to Abraham, Isaac, and Jacob (Genesis 17:8, 26:2-4, 35:12).

Jacob had never forgotten the promise given by God. Also, it wasn't something easy to leave his roots and the lands of his livelihood and go down to Egypt. But if he stayed in Canaan, it was going to be very difficult for him to survive the severe famine. He initially thought he'd go down to Egypt just for a while to avoid the famine and to meet Joseph, and then return to Canaan.

Jacob left Hebron and set out for Egypt. When he arrived at Beersheba, he offered a sacrifice before God. He wanted to remember his past and find out what God's will was by offering the sacrifice. Going down to Egypt with all his possessions was such a big event in his life. And at this moment, he reminisced over his past days.

He remembered all the delicate touches of God who had guided his life thus far and offered a sacrifice of thanksgiving. He remembered leaving home to run away from his brother Esau; working day and night at his uncle Laban's house; returning home with so much wealth given by the blessing of God; crying out to God until his thigh was dislocated before he met Esau again; and all the moments he had after settling down in Canaan.

Now, he asked God if it was His will to move to Egypt. Of course, it might have been better if he had asked before his departure, but there was a spiritual reason why he offered a sacrifice at Beersheba.

Beersheba was the place where he lived with his father Isaac before he left to uncle Laban's house to run away from his brother Esau. Also, it was the place where God appeared to Isaac and blessed him saying, *"I will bless you, and multiply your descendants, for the sake of My servant Abraham"* (Genesis 26:24).

In Genesis 21 and 26, Abraham and Isaac respectively quarreled with Abimelech, the Philistine king. Abraham planted a tamarisk tree and called on the name of the LORD, the Everlasting God. Beersheba held important meanings for Abraham and Isaac, where they used the wells as the sign of God's covenant.

Jacob remembered God's covenant at Beersheba and offered the sacrifice. We can see his faith; he kept God's covenant and its spiritual meaning deep in his heart. He wasn't completely after God's heart, but he always remembered God in his mind and sought Him.

Also, Jacob had firm faith that God would surely fulfill the dream and vision that He had given him. A long time had passed since God had made His covenant with him. But Jacob, without fail, kept in mind and believed God's promise that He would make a big nation through him and give him the land of Canaan. Because he had unwavering faith in God's promise, he relied on God at each important moment and received answers.

God accepted the sacrifice of Jacob offered at Beersheba. He appeared in a vision at night and clearly told him His will: "I am

God, the God of your father; do not be afraid to go down to Egypt, for I will make you a great nation there. I will go down with you to Egypt, and I will also surely bring you up again; and Joseph will close your eyes."

It meant Jacob's going down to Egypt was in God's providence. Also, it meant God would certainly accomplish His promise He had given to Abraham, Isaac, and then Jacob. God said He would be with Jacob and eventually He would bring him back to the Promised Land of Canaan.

Also, God let him know that it was His will for Jacob to meet Joseph and face his physical death in Joseph's presence. After receiving this clear answer, Jacob headed to Egypt in peace, along with all his household and possessions.

2. Jacob's Household Moved to Egypt

Now these are the names of the sons of Israel, Jacob and his sons, who went to Egypt: Reuben, Jacob's firstborn. The sons of Reuben: Hanoch and Pallu and Hezron and Carmi. The sons of Simeon: Jemuel and Jamin and Ohad and Jachin and Zohar and Shaul the son of a Canaanite woman. The sons of Levi: Gershon, Kohath, and Merari. The sons of Judah: Er and Onan and Shelah and Perez and Zerah (but Er and Onan died in the land of Canaan). And the sons of Perez were Hezron and Hamul. The sons of Issachar: Tola and Puvvah and Iob and Shimron. The sons of Zebulun: Sered and Elon and Jahleel. These are the sons of Leah, whom she bore to Jacob in Paddan-aram, with his daughter Dinah; all his sons and his daughters numbered thirty-three. The sons of Gad: Ziphion and Haggi, Shuni and Ezbon, Eri and Arodi and Areli. The sons of Asher: Imnah and Ishvah and Ishvi and Beriah and their sister Serah. And the sons of Beriah: Heber and Malchiel. These are the sons of Zilpah, whom Laban gave to his daughter Leah; and she bore to Jacob these sixteen persons. The sons of Jacob's wife Rachel: Joseph and Benjamin. Now to Joseph in the land of Egypt were born Manasseh and Ephraim, whom Asenath, the daughter of Potiphera, priest of On, bore to him. The sons of Benjamin: Bela and Becher and Ashbel, Gera and Naaman, Ehi and Rosh, Muppim and Huppim and Ard. These are the sons of Rachel, who were born to Jacob; there were fourteen persons in all. The sons of Dan: Hushim. The sons of Naphtali: Jahzeel and Guni and Jezer and Shillem. These are the sons of Bilhah, whom Laban gave to his daughter Rachel, and she bore these to Jacob; there were seven persons in all. All the persons belonging to Jacob, who came to Egypt, his direct descendants, not including the wives of Jacob's sons, were sixty-six persons in all, and the sons of Joseph, who were born to him in Egypt were two; all the persons of the house of Jacob, who came to Egypt, were seventy. (46:8-27)

Jacob's family that moved to Egypt included his eleven sons and their wives; and their children and also the herds and flocks. It must have been quite a number of people, and a great volume of luggage and animals moved together, with the little ones and women on wagons. The Bible records the genealogy around the twelve sons of Jacob, according to the mother's names.

Reuben, born of Leah, had four sons. Reuben's first son Hanoch became the father of the family of Hanoch. Pallu and Hezron and Carmi also became the father of their respective families (Numbers 26:5-6).

Leah's second son Simeon had six sons: Jemuel and Jamin and Ohad and Jachin and Zohar and Shaul. They, too, became the fathers of their respective families (Numbers 26:12-13). Leah's third son Levi had three sons.

Leah's fourth son Judah had five sons. The sons Judah begot with the Canaanite wife were Er and Onan and Shelah. Er and Onan were evil before God and they died in Canaan (Genesis 38:7-10). So, in order to continue the family line, Tamar cheated Judah her father-in-law and gave birth to Judah's sons Perez and Zerah. They were twins. Perez later had two sons Hezron and Hamul.

Leah's fifth son Issachar had four sons: Tola and Puvvah and Iob and Shimron. Leah's sixth son Zebulun had three sons: Sered and Elon and Jahleel. The number of Jacob's children that he begot with Leah was 33, including his daughter Dinah, six sons, and their children.

Next, the number of Jacob's children that Jacob begot with Zilpah, maid of Leah, was 16. Zilpah gave birth to Gad and Asher. Gad had seven sons. Asher had four sons and a daughter. Asher's son Beriah had two sons.

Jacob's most beloved wife Rachel gave birth to Joseph and Benjamin. Joseph married Asenath, the daughter of Potiphera, priest of On, and begot Manasseh and Ephraim. Jacob's last son Benjamin had ten sons, so the number of children between Jacob and Rachel were 14. Rachel gave her maid Bilhah to Jacob, and she bore Dan and Naphtali. Dan begot Hushim, and Naphtali begot Jahzeel and Guni and Jezer and Shillem. Thus, the number of children between Jacob and Bilhah was 7.

In all, Jacob's children who settled in Egypt were 70 people including Joseph and his sons.

3. When Pharaoh Calls You and Says, 'What is Your Occupation?'

Now he sent Judah before him to Joseph, to point out the way before him to Goshen; and they came into the land of Goshen. Joseph prepared his chariot and went up to Goshen to meet his father Israel; as soon as he appeared before him, he fell on his neck and wept on his neck a long time. Then Israel said to Joseph, "Now let me die, since I have seen your face, that you are still alive." Joseph said to his brothers and to his father's household, "I will go up and tell Pharaoh, and will say to him, 'My brothers and my father's household, who were in the land of Canaan, have come to me; and the men are shepherds, for they have been keepers of livestock; and they have brought their flocks and their herds and all that they have.' When Pharaoh calls you and says, 'What is your occupation?' you shall say, 'Your servants have been keepers of livestock from our youth even until now, both we and our fathers,' that you may live in the land of Goshen; for every shepherd is loathsome to the Egyptians." (46:28-34)

Jacob and his household finally arrived in Egypt. Jacob sent Judah before him to Joseph to let him know of their arrival. Joseph appeared before Jacob in a dignified form, riding his chariot. What would they have felt at this reunion?

They must have had deep emotions for they had spent 22 long years having earnest yearning for each other. Especially for Jacob, he received his son back who he thought had been dead. How happy he must have been! They tearfully hugged each other. Jacob had no more wishes and he could die satisfied right now.

After this touching reunion of the father and the son, Joseph said he would inform the Pharaoh that his father and family came. Joseph already knew what he had to say to Pharaoh for his family to continue their business and prosper in a stable and independent environment.

For this reason he advised his brothers and his father's household that, if the king asked what they did for a living, they were to say they were keepers of livestock. It was not just some shallow methodology coming out from a cunning mind to serve his interests. He received a precise urging of God as to what he had to do in order to fulfill God's will and providence.

If Jacob's household asked them to let them work in a field or industry that the Egyptians considered important, it'd have been somewhat burdensome for the Egyptians and the Pharaoh. They might even be alerted thinking they could suffer a loss. But because keeping the livestock was something they considered loathsome, they could easily let Jacob's household live in Goshen without keeping them in check.

Considering something 'loathsome' is to consider it trifling and insignificant. Keeping the livestock was considered a lowly job in Egypt. There was another reason why they said they were keepers of livestock knowing the fact that the Egyptians considered it loathsome. It's to set some distance from them.

One of the important tasks for Israel living in Egypt was to keep their identity as the Elect of God. They had to keep themselves from intermarrying and idolatry. If they intermarried and accepted Egyptian culture, they could soon lose God's covenant. For this reason they said they were the keepers of livestock to be separated from the Egyptians.

But a more fundamental reason why Joseph advised his brothers what to say before the king was that he knew the king's mind. Pharaoh was a kind of person who would pay back the grace and who had some goodness. But he was not a man of truth. He could change his mind anytime with the passage of time and if something was not beneficial for him.

Right now, he was grateful to Joseph, so he wanted to grant anything that Joseph and his family asked. But he could regret or even overturn his decision later. Knowing this very well, Joseph came up with a way so that there would be no problem later.

At the same time, Joseph advised his brothers to ask Pharaoh in a way that was very easy for him to accept. He knew all the situations of Egypt clearly, and he knew exactly in which place his father and his household had to settle down.

Here, we should learn the wisdom of goodness. With regard to getting what he wanted, Joseph pursued peace and did not have any conflict with anybody. It was because he had wisdom of goodness. He made others feel comfortable and gained the understanding from God of the way that was beneficial for everyone.

Even if they understand others' hearts, those who have wisdom of goodness do not misuse their understanding for their own benefit. They do everything to make it good for everybody. Only those who have the wisdom given by God from above, the wisdom that comes out from the heart of goodness and truth, can give happiness to everyone and not just themselves.

Add-in 4

The Promised Land of Canaan Given to Abraham, Isaac, and Jacob

1. The Covenant God made with Abraham(Abram)

"Now the LORD said to Abram, 'Go forth from your country, and from your relatives and from your father's house, to the land which I will show you; and I will make you a great nation, and I will bless you, and make your name great; and so you shall be a blessing; and I will bless those who bless you, and the one who curses you I will curse. And in you all the families of the earth will be blessed.'" (Genesis 12:1-3)

"Abram took Sarai, his wife; his nephew, Lot; all their possessions which they had accumulated; and the persons which they had acquired in Haran and they set out for the land of Canaan. They came to the land of Canaan. Abram passed through the land as far as the site of Shechem, to the oak of Moreh. Now the Canaanite was then in the land. The LORD appeared to Abram and said, 'To your descendants I will give this land.' So he built an altar there to the LORD who had appeared to him." (Genesis 12:5-7)

"And He said to him, 'I am the LORD who brought you out of Ur of the Chaldeans, to give you this land to possess it.'" (Genesis 15:7)

"I will give to you and to your descendants after you, the land of your sojournings, all the land of Canaan, for an everlasting possession; and I will be their God." (Genesis 17:8)

2. The Promise Given to Isaac

"The LORD appeared to him and said, 'Do not go down to Egypt; stay in the land of which I shall tell you. Sojourn in this land and I will be with you and bless you, for to you and to your descendants I will give all these lands, and I will establish the oath which I swore to your father Abraham. I will multiply your descendants as the stars of heaven, and will give your descendants all these lands; and by your descendants all the nations of the earth shall be blessed.'" (Genesis 26:2-4)

3. The Promise Given to Jacob

"He had a dream, and behold, a ladder was set on the earth with its top reaching to heaven; and behold, the angels of God were ascending and descending on it. And behold, the LORD stood above it and said, 'I am the LORD, the God of your father Abraham and the God of Isaac; the land on which you lie, I will give it to you and to your descendants. Your descendants will also be like the dust of the earth, and you will spread out to the west and to the east and to the north and to the south; and in you and in your descendants shall all the families of the earth be blessed. Behold, I am with you and will keep you wherever you go, and will bring you back to this land; for I will not leave you until I have done what I have promised you.'" (Genesis 28:12-15)

"Then God appeared to Jacob again when he came from Paddan-aram, and He blessed him. God said to him, 'Your name is Jacob; You shall no longer be called Jacob, but Israel shall be your name.' Thus He called him Israel. God also said to him, 'I am God Almighty; be fruitful and multiply; a nation and a company of nations shall come from you, and kings shall come forth from you. The land which I gave to Abraham and Isaac, I will give it to you, and I will give the land to your descendants after you.'" (Genesis 35:9-12)

"He said, 'I am God, the God of your father; do not be afraid to go down to Egypt, for I will make you a great nation there. I will go down with you to Egypt, and I will also surely bring you up again; and Joseph will close your eyes.'" (Genesis 46:3-4)

Joseph
Chapter 9

Joseph's Wisdom of Goodness and Policies for Famine

Joseph Considers All Details from Pharaoh's Perspective

Getting Rameses through Joseph's Wisdom

Joseph Deals with the Deepening Famine

New Land Policy of Egypt

Vowing to Bury Jacob in His Fathers' Burial Place

1. Joseph Considers All Details from Pharaoh's Perspective

Then Joseph went in and told Pharaoh, and said, "My father and my brothers and their flocks and their herds and all that they have, have come out of the land of Canaan; and behold, they are in the land of Goshen." He took five men from among his brothers and presented them to Pharaoh. Then Pharaoh said to his brothers, "What is your occupation?" So they said to Pharaoh, "Your servants are shepherds, both we and our fathers." They said to Pharaoh, "We have come to sojourn in the land, for there is no pasture for your servants' flocks, for the famine is severe in the land of Canaan. Now, therefore, please let your servants live in the land of Goshen." Then Pharaoh said to Joseph, "Your father and your brothers have come to you. The land of Egypt is at your disposal; settle your father and your brothers in the best of the land, let them live in the land of Goshen; and if you know any capable men among them, then put them in charge of my livestock." (47:1-6)

From the start Joseph considered the land of Goshen as the place for his family to settle down. Goshen was a remote area and had little of the Egyptians' influence so that Joseph's family would be better able to keep their blood and identity there. It was also good pasture land for keeping the livestock. Joseph let his family stay in Goshen temporarily, and then acted wisely so that the Pharaoh would willfully give them the land.

He reported to the king saying, "My father and my brothers and their flocks and their herds and all that they have, have come out of the land of Canaan; and behold, they are in the land of Goshen." Informing the king about his family's arrival, he intentionally mentioned that they had the herds and the flocks.

By saying that they were shepherds, an occupation considered loathsome to the Egyptians, Joseph wanted to let the king understand that his family wouldn't be any threat to Egypt. Also, saying they were in Goshen meant that they were waiting for the order of Pharaoh from their temporary settlement in Goshen.

If he said, "My family wants to settle down in Goshen," or "I hope my family can stay in Goshen," then it could be considered the same as informing him and not asking for permission. But because he had respect for Pharaoh, Joseph spoke in a very considerate way so that he could let Pharaoh make the decision while letting the king know that Goshen was the right place to give to his family. The king could entrust everything to Joseph because he had this kind of humility, service, and consideration.

After reporting to Pharaoh of the arrival of his family, Joseph selected only five of his brothers to show to Pharaoh. Why did he do so? It was because if all twelve brothers appeared before the king, it could be conceived as a kind of threat and make Pharaoh nervous.

Of course, Pharaoh already heard and knew Joseph had ten older brothers and the total number of his household is 70. But if ten men show up at the same time, what the king would actually feel could be different from just hearing about them. Joseph selected only five of them so that Pharaoh wouldn't have even the slightest bit of negative feelings about his family.

Joseph always thought from the viewpoint of Pharaoh and considered every detail of all the matters. It doesn't mean Joseph thought he could move the heart of Pharaoh through his own wisdom and methods. All his actions came out from the faith in and dependence on God. He never relied on human wisdom, including his own.

He did all his best in every matter, but he committed everything into God's hands when it came down to the process and result. For this reason God gave him wisdom according to his faith and moved the heart of Pharaoh to make all situations smooth.

Finally, Pharaoh and Joseph's brothers met each other. As Joseph anticipated, the king first asked them their occupation. Joseph could anticipate Pharaoh's question because he understood the personality and interests of the Pharaoh precisely. Based on this understanding, he could assist the king and take care of the administration of the country before any problem could arise. . It was not a result that he could get just because he had extensive knowledge and ability to analyze the situations.

For example, those who are very intelligent and have a great deal of hands-on experiences can see clearly the ways to take care of their jobs. But the result can be very different depending on the kind of relationships they maintain with coworkers and the extent to which they behave with virtue and humbleness. If they don't maintain peace with others, they can't get any help from God, and they can't expect great results. Even if they get good results, they can be considered as hard-working and intelligent persons, but not necessarily as respectable and trustworthy persons.

Joseph had not only the knowledge and experience to read all the situations around him, but he also had the wisdom of goodness to gain and move the hearts of other people. He understood the Pharaoh's heart with this wisdom of goodness so that without any burdensome feelings the king would grant him what he desired.

And Joseph's brothers answered Pharaoh exactly as Joseph had advised them to: "Your servants are shepherds, both we and our fathers. We have come to sojourn in the land, for there is no pasture for your servants' flocks, for the famine is severe in the land of Canaan. Now, therefore, please let your servants live in the land of Goshen."

They said they came there to seek the grace of the Pharaoh due to the inevitable situation, famine. It means they didn't come there to take something from the fertile land of Egypt. And very humbly they asked the king to allow them to settle down in Goshen.

Pharaoh already received the report that they were temporarily staying in Goshen, and he was also aware that Goshen was a good land for keeping the livestock. Also, in the viewpoint of the king, there was nothing threatening about Joseph's brothers. Pharaoh thought they'd just quietly keep the livestock and serve him, so he generously accepted their request.

He showed the generosity of the ruler saying, "The land of Egypt is at your disposal; settle your father and your brothers in the best of the land, let them live in the land of Goshen." Furthermore, he gave them a duty to take care of his livestock, too. Truly it was a gesture of great trust and generosity to allow foreigners to take care of the king's possessions.

2. Getting Rameses through Joseph's Wisdom

Then Joseph brought his father Jacob and presented him to Pharaoh; and Jacob blessed Pharaoh. Pharaoh said to Jacob, "How many years have you lived?" So Jacob said to Pharaoh, "The years of my sojourning are one hundred and thirty; few and unpleasant have been the years of my life, nor have they attained the years that my fathers lived during the days of their sojourning." And Jacob blessed Pharaoh, and went out from his presence. So Joseph settled his father and his brothers and gave them a possession in the land of Egypt, in the best of the land, in the land of Rameses, as Pharaoh had ordered. Joseph provided his father and his brothers and all his father's household with food, according to their little ones. (47:7-12)

After he received the permission of the king for his family's settlement, Joseph brought his father Jacob before Pharaoh. He did so in order to set the distinction between his father and the brothers.

Also, it was to avoid any uncomfortable situation that could have happened to his father Jacob. Joseph did not introduce his father while he didn't know how the king would react and while he couldn't be certain of whether or not they could get the land they wanted. He introduced his father when he got all the permissions from the king and everything was at ease. The king also was in comfort after meeting Joseph's brothers, and he treated Jacob well. We can see this from the scene where Jacob was blessing Pharaoh.

Pharaoh did not feel offended because a mere tribal leader blessed him. Also, he didn't have any problem although Jacob did not bless him in the name of the god that he served. He just thought Jacob was a very old man, the father of his beloved servant, and accepted his blessing pleasingly. It means his mind was open.

When Pharaoh asked him his age, Jacob replied, "The years of my sojourning are one hundred and thirty; few and unpleasant have been the years of my life, nor have they attained the years that my fathers lived during the days of their sojourning."

Jacob's reply reaffirmed that Jacob and his household was not a threat to Pharaoh at all. Pharaoh came to think that Jacob and his fathers had been nomads for a very long time, and they wouldn't try to conquer or take any other people's land.

Jacob's family had a pleasant meeting with Pharaoh. They were guaranteed a settlement in Goshen by the wisdom of Joseph. Now, Joseph could support his family in the stable and comfortable environment.

What if Joseph at his discretion let his father and brothers have the land of Goshen without going through official procedures? Even though Egypt was in great debt to Joseph, some people would complain about it, and even think Jacob's family was enjoying good things with the taxes they had paid.

However, Joseph's supporting his family was approved by the Pharaoh. Nobody had anything to say about it. Joseph gave Rameses to his father Jacob and brothers according to the command of Pharaoh. Rameses is the name of an old city in Goshen.

The more we come to know about Joseph, the more we can feel his wisdom was great. We can't help but feel amazed by the fact that he foresaw what would come as if he had seen it and that he moved the hearts of other people as he intended.

What we have to understand here is that his wisdom was not used with a self-centered ulterior motive to use other people for his own interest. One cannot out of evil heart show wisdom of goodness to move the heart of others. Although he was the most beloved servant of Pharaoh, he never broke the order of things. But instead, he always considered and respected others first, and this is the reason why he could see the clear way of goodness.

Also, Pharaoh's heart was not moved just by a couple of words of Joseph. Pharaoh had observed Joseph for a long time seeing how faithful and selfless Joseph was. He knew Joseph really served him with all his heart. Pharaoh granted Joseph's request based on this trust.

And all these things were done by the providence of God. Joseph didn't guide his family to Goshen out of a mere personal affection. He did so bravely because he was precisely inspired by God as to what he had to do to lay the foundation of the nation of Israel.

3. Joseph Deals with the Deepening Famine

Now there was no food in all the land, because the famine was very severe, so that the land of Egypt and the land of Canaan languished because of the famine. Joseph gathered all the money that was found in the land of Egypt and in the land of Canaan for the grain which they bought, and Joseph brought the money into Pharaoh's house. When the money was all spent in the land of Egypt and in the land of Canaan, all the Egyptians came to Joseph and said, "Give us food, for why should we die in your presence? For our money is gone." Then Joseph said, "Give up your livestock, and I will give you food for your livestock, since your money is gone." So they brought their livestock to Joseph, and Joseph gave them food in exchange for the horses and the flocks and the herds and the donkeys; and he fed them with food in exchange for all their livestock that year. When that year was ended, they came to him the next year and said to him, "We will not hide from my lord that our money is all spent, and the cattle are my lord's. There is nothing left for my lord except our bodies and our lands. "Why should we die before your eyes, both we and our land? Buy us and our land for food, and we and our land will be slaves to Pharaoh. So give us seed, that we may live and not die, and that the land may not be desolate." (47:13-19)

So many lives are lost due to the hunger in times of famine even in this modern world with developed civilization. If the worst kind of drought continues, the crops and grass will dry up and many people and cattle will starve. Today, we have some international relief and aid but famine was something truly fearful thousands of years ago. If the whole region was affected and the neighboring countries were also suffering from the same famine, there couldn't have been any solution.

But Joseph received the wisdom of God, and he overcame the seven-year famine in Egypt. He made all the preparations during the seven years of abundance, and they had grain in the storehouses in Egypt even during the harshness of the famine.

This grain was the lifeline not only for the Egyptians but also for the people of neighboring countries. Those people who had no more food began to buy the food with money. Egypt became rich with this money. But the famine continued even after all the money in Egypt and Canaan land ran out.

As they had no more money, people asked Joseph to give them grain for free. Joseph suggested they exchange their livestock for grain, and they willingly accepted the proposal. In fact it was burdensome for them to take care of the livestock since they didn't have enough food for themselves.

After a year, they wouldn't even have any livestock and they had nothing to pay for the grain. Now, the people said they would die and the lands would become desolate, and they asked Joseph to buy their bodies and their lands. They said they'd be slaves of Pharaoh and they'd farm his lands in return for receiving grain.

4. New Land Policy of Egypt

So Joseph bought all the land of Egypt for Pharaoh, for every Egyptian sold his field, because the famine was severe upon them. Thus the land became Pharaoh's. As for the people, he removed them to the cities from one end of Egypt's border to the other. Only the land of the priests he did not buy, for the priests had an allotment from Pharaoh, and they lived off the allotment which Pharaoh gave them. Therefore, they did not sell their land. Then Joseph said to the people, "Behold, I have today bought you and your land for Pharaoh; now, here is seed for you, and you may sow the land. At the harvest you shall give a fifth to Pharaoh, and four-fifths shall be your own for seed of the field and for your food and for those of your households and as food for your little ones." So they said, "You have saved our lives! Let us find favor in the sight of my lord, and we will be Pharaoh's slaves." Joseph made it a statute concerning the land of Egypt valid to this day, that Pharaoh should have the fifth; only the land of the priests did not become Pharaoh's. (47:20-26)

Joseph bought all the land and the land became Pharaoh's. As for the people, they became tenant farmers. This might seem Joseph's policies were cold-hearted. He already had so much grain in store, and he could have just given it to the people for free. But he bought all their livestock, land, and their bodies and caused them to belong to Pharaoh.

But what if Joseph just gave the food away? Then, people would have easily wasted food thinking that if the food ran out they could just go to Joseph and ask him for food. This way, even if there was a great amount of food in the stores, it would have been difficult for them to endure the famine.

Joseph avoided any waste of food by taking a price for it from the people. That doesn't mean he overcharged. He didn't ask for something impossible when he made the people tenant farmers to farm Pharaoh's land. They were to give to Pharaoh a fifth or 20% of the harvest and they could keep the rest for their seeds and their food. We can understand this was a very reasonable deal when we read what the people said to Joseph. They asked him to make them slaves saying, "You have saved our lives! Let us find favor in the sight of my lord, and we will be Pharaoh's slaves."

What if Joseph's methodology in dealing with the famine had been unfair? The people who were already in trouble could have had complaints and even revolted. They might have complained against Joseph saying, "He took away our money, livestock, and land, and he is making us slaves now." But they said that Joseph had saved their lives and they were in great debt. They were thankful to him. Joseph maintained the economy of the country by overcoming the famine successfully, and at the same time he made Pharaoh very rich.

There was another policy that showed Joseph's wisdom. He excluded the land of the priests when he was buying the land. Priests belonged to Pharaoh and received their allotments from Pharaoh. It was to honor the authority of Pharaoh that Joseph didn't buy the land of the priests.

If Joseph lacked wisdom but was only full of enthusiasm, he could have bought the land of the priests and made them Pharaoh's. He could have thought this would satisfy Pharaoh, but actually it could have been posing a threat to Joseph himself. Why is it so?

Joseph married the daughter of a priest by the arrangement of Pharaoh when he was appointed the prime minister. But he never worshipped idols. He only served the LORD God. And yet, because his behaviors were humble and he was trusted by Pharaoh completely, other people just looked the other way about it. If Joseph dealt with the possessions of the priests, it could have caused religious conflict.

People might have thought, 'He is despising the priests because he despises the god of Egypt!' Joseph knew there was room for such a dispute and he did not cross any line that he shouldn't have crossed. He honored the part that already belonged to Pharaoh and maintained trust with him.

Egypt endured the famine very well thanks to this wise Joseph. Pharaoh solidified his power without any effort, and the national power also increased. To Pharaoh, Joseph was a very precious minister who brought the country out of a potentially fatal crisis. He was an asset that was absolutely indispensable. Furthermore, he honored the king without any change in his attitude. He was humble and good, and he had no fault in him. For this reason Pharaoh lifted him up to the highest degree he could.

5. Vowing to Bury Jacob in His Fathers' Burial Place

Now Israel lived in the land of Egypt, in Goshen, and they acquired property in it and were fruitful and became very numerous. Jacob lived in the land of Egypt seventeen years; so the length of Jacob's life was one hundred and forty-seven years. When the time for Israel to die drew near, he called his son Joseph and said to him, "Please, if I have found favor in your sight, place now your hand under my thigh and deal with me in kindness and faithfulness. Please do not bury me in Egypt, but when I lie down with my fathers, you shall carry me out of Egypt and bury me in their burial place." And he said, "I will do as you have said." He said, "Swear to me." So he swore to him. Then Israel bowed in worship at the head of the bed. (47:27-31)

While Joseph was ruling Egypt, his father and his children multiplied in Goshen, enjoying affluent lives. It shows God's covenant that had been given to Abraham, Isaac, and Jacob was being fulfilled.

Now, 17 years passed since Jacob had moved to Egypt. He lived a happy life since his reunion with Joseph in Egypt. Why would God allow Jacob 17 years of life in Egypt?

It was after 22 years that Joseph met his father who had loved him so very much. And what would he feel if his father died in just a couple of years? He'd have felt very sorry and heartbroken for not having been able to honor and serve him enough because his father had been in great pain for so many years through him.

Considering this heart of Joseph, God let him be with his father for 17 years. The number 17 has the spiritual meaning that "God Himself is in control and He is acting."

Just as it was in the providence of God that Joseph was sold into Egypt when he was 17, it was also God's plan that Jacob and Joseph could spent 17 years together after the reunion. It was a happy time both for Joseph and Jacob.

Jacob not only took rest in physical sense, but he gained benefit in spiritual sense. Seeing the wise decisions and behaviors of Joseph, he came to realize his shortcomings one by one. Especially when he thought Joseph might have died, he didn't rely on God but fell into despair saying, *"Surely I will go down to Sheol in mourning for my son."* He was very sorry for this before God.

Jacob now knew he was going to die and made Joseph vow. He said, "Please, if I have found favor in your sight, place now your hand under my thigh and deal with me in kindness and faithfulness. Please do not bury me in Egypt, but when I lie down with my fathers, you shall carry me out of Egypt and bury me in their burial place."

'Thigh' spiritually symbolizes 'uprightness and being unchanging'. To make a vow with the hands under the thigh is to announce the vow before God and to commit it to God so that He would guarantee and fulfill it.

What is the reason that Jacob wanted to be buried where his fathers were buried, even by making Joseph make such a vow? It's because he had the faith and hope that God would let his descendants form a great nation in the land of Canaan, which was a dream and vision given by God.

Jacob had an inner heart that wouldn't forget God's promise even after a very long time and even though circumstances were different. He faithfully believed in God's promise until his death, and he wanted to prove his trust by being buried where his fathers were buried. His faith in God's promise was rock-solid.

The same goes for Joseph. He was sold into Egypt at a young age, but he never forgot God's promise that he had learned from his father. Joseph didn't follow Jacob's last will merely out of his love for his father; he also had the same hope and faith that Jacob did and made a promise to bury him where their fathers were buried.

Considering his upright heart, God established Jacob as the father of Israel and laid the foundation of Israel through his son Joseph in Egypt.

Joseph
Chapter 10

Joseph's Sons, Manasseh and Ephraim

Joseph Sees Jacob at His Deathbed

Jacob Blesses Joseph's Sons

Jacob Puts Ephraim before Manasseh

Jacob Gives More Inheritance to Joseph

1. Joseph Sees Jacob at His Deathbed

Now it came about after these things that Joseph was told, "Behold, your father is sick." So he took his two sons Manasseh and Ephraim with him. When it was told to Jacob, "Behold, your son Joseph has come to you," Israel collected his strength and sat up in the bed. Then Jacob said to Joseph, "God Almighty appeared to me at Luz in the land of Canaan and blessed me, and He said to me, 'Behold, I will make you fruitful and numerous, and I will make you a company of peoples, and will give this land to your descendants after you for an everlasting possession.' Now your two sons, who were born to you in the land of Egypt before I came to you in Egypt, are mine; Ephraim and Manasseh shall be mine, as Reuben and Simeon are. But your offspring that have been born after them shall be yours; they shall be called by the names of their brothers in their inheritance. Now as for me, when I came from Paddan, Rachel died, to my sorrow, in the land of Canaan on the journey, when there was still some distance to go to Ephrath; and I buried her there on the way to Ephrath (that is, Bethlehem)." (48:1-7)

In the face of the national crisis of severe famine, Joseph dealt with it perfectly in all aspects as the prime minister. Especially, since his family had come to dwell in Goshen, he tried even more to do his best taking care of all the national matters.

If Joseph neglected his job just a little bit taking care of his family, then Pharaoh and his servants would not have deemed it favorable. They might have misunderstood him thinking, 'His hardwork until now was just to bring his family here and make them rich!' Predicting such a reaction very well, he dedicated himself even more to his job to avoid any problems that might have arisen due to his family. Thanks to his hard efforts, Pharaoh and his servants thought the presence of Joseph's family was beneficial for them.

That doesn't mean Joseph neglected his family. He managed all his duties to his family while performing his job as the prime minister. We can easily imagine he did all his best to serve his father in order to compensate his father for the 22 years that had been lost. But Joseph did not cause any discomfort to others just to serve his father; he always followed the way of justice, and he never neglected any of his jobs.

One day Joseph heard his father, Jacob, was sick. He brought his two sons, Manasseh and Ephraim, to his father. We should pay attention to one thing here.

It is said, "Joseph was told," and "it was told to Jacob." It means somebody was telling them the news. We can see that there was a person like a messenger who was travelling between Joseph and his family in Goshen.

Joseph always heard from this person about the well-being of his father and his household. If they needed anything, he knew it in detail and provided them with what they needed. Having a messenger, he could take care of his family discreetly, without making anybody uncomfortable.

Here, saying that Jacob was sick was in the words of the messenger. Of course, Jacob was old and weak, and he couldn't see well. But he had no disease. It's just that he was very weak because of his age. He couldn't move around freely and he had to lie down on his bed. Seeing this, the messenger said that Jacob was 'sick'.

Both Jacob's and his father Isaac's eyes 'became dim' and they became weaker in old age because they didn't take after God's heart completely. Deuteronomy 34:7 says, *"Although Moses was one hundred and twenty years old when he died, his eye was not dim, nor his vigor abated."* The reason why God recorded how Moses was just before he died is to let us know what kind of physical condition one will have before death if he resembles God completely.

We can say Isaac and Jacob died peacefully. But, facing death with a weak body and weak bodily functions, and facing death due to God's taking away the life-force after having perfect and complete health until the final moment, as in the case of Moses, are very different from each other.

Jacob was weak, but when he heard Joseph had come, he gathered his strength and sat up. He explained to Joseph about the covenant that God had given him.

God had appeared to him in Luz, namely Bethel, and said to

him, *"I am God Almighty; be fruitful and multiply; a nation and a company of nations shall come from you, and kings shall come forth from you. The land which I gave to Abraham and Isaac, I will give it to you, and I will give the land to your descendants after you"* (Genesis 35:11-12).

About Joseph's two sons Ephraim and Manasseh, Jacob said, they were his. It means he would treat his grandsons Ephraim and Manasseh as his sons. Jacob let Joseph's two sons come into the covenant of God that would be fulfilled through him.

He continued to say, "But your offspring that have been born after them shall be yours; they shall be called by the names of their brothers in their inheritance." Jacob included not only Joseph's two sons but also their descendants to come into the covenant of blessing. It means the blessing that would be given to Manasseh and Ephraim would be given to their descendants as well.

Then, Jacob suddenly mentioned Rachel. He said, "Now as for me, when I came from Paddan, Rachel died, to my sorrow, in the land of Canaan on the journey, when there was still some distance to go to Ephrath; and I buried her there on the way to Ephrath (that is, Bethlehem)."

The reason why he said this at his deathbed was to express how much he loved Rachel; how pleased he was when Rachel gave birth to Joseph; and how much he loved Joseph. Jacob reminded Joseph and his two grandsons of the burial place of Rachel. It was to advise them to remember their ancestors in their lives.

We can feel that Rachel took up such a big part in Jacob's heart in 147 years of his life. Even after such a very long time, he still had unchanging love for Rachel.

2. Jacob Blesses Joseph's Sons

When Israel saw Joseph's sons, he said, "Who are these?" Joseph said to his father, "They are my sons, whom God has given me here." So he said, "Bring them to me, please, that I may bless them." Now the eyes of Israel were so dim from age that he could not see. Then Joseph brought them close to him, and he kissed them and embraced them. Israel said to Joseph, "I never expected to see your face, and behold, God has let me see your children as well." Then Joseph took them from his knees, and bowed with his face to the ground. Joseph took them both, Ephraim with his right hand toward Israel's left, and Manasseh with his left hand toward Israel's right, and brought them close to him. But Israel stretched out his right hand and laid it on the head of Ephraim, who was the younger, and his left hand on Manasseh's head, crossing his hands, although Manasseh was the firstborn. He blessed Joseph, and said, "The God before whom my fathers Abraham and Isaac walked, the God who has been my shepherd all my life to this day, the angel who has redeemed me from all evil, bless the lads; and may my name live on in them, and the names of my fathers Abraham and Isaac; and may they grow into a multitude in the midst of the earth." (48:8-16)

Seeing Joseph's sons, Jacob asked Joseph who they were, not because he didn't know who they were but because he wanted to hear from Joseph directly. If Joseph had his own opinion about it, he might have thought, 'My father doesn't recognize his grandsons as he is very old.' But Joseph knew exactly why Jacob asked such a question, and he replied, "They are my sons, whom God has given me here."

He didn't just say they were his sons but they were his sons whom God had given him. He wanted to point out that, although they were born in Egypt, they were given by God, and therefore, they were still in God's covenant given to Abraham, Isaac, and Jacob.

We should consider one thing here. It's that we can give the right answer when we fully understand the intention in the question that is asked.

In Mark chapter 5, we read about a woman who had bled for 12 years. She touched the edge of Jesus' robe and was healed of her disease. Then, Jesus knew power went out from Him and asked, "Who touched My garments?" He read the good heart of the woman believing that she would be healed just by touching His garments. He wanted to reveal her heart and heal her completely.

But the disciples didn't understand His intention in His question and replied, "You see the crowd pressing in on You, and You say, 'Who touched Me?'" They meant to say, "There are so many people pushing each other and anybody could have touched Your garments, and why would You ask who touched Your garments?" They were thinking and responding as though Jesus didn't understand the situation.

What if the disciples had been spiritually awake? They most likely would have thought, 'Jesus knows the situation, so, He must have a reason to ask such a question.'

Joseph understood his father's intention in his question: Jacob wanted to bless Joseph who was doing the role of the spiritual firstborn and his two sons. So, as Jacob told him, "Bring them to me, please." Joseph brought his two sons before Jacob.

Jacob kissed them, embraced them, and expressed his joy to Joseph, "I never expected to see your face, and behold, God has let me see your children as well."

Now Joseph took them from his knees, and bowed with his face to the ground. Then, he brought his two sons before Jacob so that he could bless Manasseh, the first son, with his right hand, and Ephraim the second son with his left hand.

The majority of people have greater strength in the right hand. In the Bible 'right hand' symbolizes authority and power (Psalm 62:8; Revelation 1:16-17, 2:1, 10:5) or strong power (Exodus 15:6; Psalm 17:7, 89:13). Also, they gave blessings with their right hand (Genesis 48:14).

Joseph thought it was right to let Manasseh the first son to receive more blessings, so he put him on the right hand of Jacob. Unexpectedly, Jacob crossed his arms to put his right hand on Ephraim and his left hand on Manasseh.

Jacob blessed his two grandsons with his arms crossed, "The

God before whom my fathers Abraham and Isaac walked, the God who has been my shepherd all my life to this day, the angel who has redeemed me from all evil, bless the lads; and may my name live on in them, and the names of my fathers Abraham and Isaac; and may they grow into a multitude in the midst of the earth"

3. Jacob Puts Ephraim before Manasseh

When Joseph saw that his father laid his right hand on Ephraim's head, it displeased him; and he grasped his father's hand to remove it from Ephraim's head to Manasseh's head. Joseph said to his father, "Not so, my father, for this one is the firstborn. Place your right hand on his head." But his father refused and said, "I know, my son, I know; he also will become a people and he also will be great. However, his younger brother shall be greater than he, and his descendants shall become a multitude of nations." He blessed them that day, saying, "By you Israel will pronounce blessing, saying, 'May God make you like Ephraim and Manasseh!'" Thus he put Ephraim before Manasseh. (48:17-20)

When Joseph saw his father put his right hand on Ephraim the second son, he asked his father to move his right hand to Manasseh. But Jacob refused saying, "I know, my son, I know; he also will become a people and he also will be great. However, his younger brother shall be greater than he, and his descendants shall become a multitude of nations."

Why did Jacob refuse Joseph's request? It's because his heart was moved by God in His providence. Of course one would think it is right to bless the first son Manasseh more greatly, but Jacob only obeyed God's urging. We can see the contrast between Jacob and Isaac. Isaac tried to bless his first son Esau, knowing very well it wasn't in accordance with God's will.

In Genesis chapter 25, Isaac knew that his second son Jacob's descendants would become greater than those of his first son Esau, and Esau would serve Jacob. And yet, Isaac loved Esau more and told him to bring him savory food to bless him.

But Rebekah became aware of Isaac's plan and she came up with her own scheme. Finally, the blessing was given to Jacob. Because of this incident Jacob had to be put in long-lasting trials. Until he was reconciled to his brother Esau, he had time to break his ego completely.

What if Isaac had followed God's will and providence? There wouldn't have been the tragedy of his two sons having enmity between them. And, because Jacob had such an experience, he intended to bless Ephraim the second son more following the urging of God alone and not any human thoughts.

Now, Joseph's spiritual level was more advanced than that of Jacob, so why is it that he was not moved by God as precisely as his father? It's because, in that situation, it wasn't Joseph but Jacob who was fulfilling the will of God. The formation of the twelve tribes of Israel was supposed to be done by Jacob. So, it was Jacob's work to bless Ephraim and Manasseh who would form a part of the twelve tribes of Israel.

For this reason God let Jacob, not Joseph, bless Ephraim and Manasseh. In other words, it's not that Joseph received a wrong inspiration of the Spirit. At that moment it was God who was moving Jacob to fulfill His will.

We can learn a very important spiritual lesson here. 1 Corinthians 14:30 says, *"But if a revelation is made to another who is seated, the first one must keep silent."* God is not a God of confusion but of peace, and He works according to the order of things.

For example, if He gives prophecy to many people, God works precisely according to the order so that those receiving the prophecy will be in harmony. Suppose you are receiving prophecy and if another person begins to receive prophecy too, you should realize that God is working through another person's lips and you should keep silent. For this reason 1 Corinthians 14:32 says, *"...and the spirits of prophets are subject to prophets."*

It's not only about prophecy. You should never say the inspiration or urging of the Spirit you received is 100% correct. It is because this means you think God is working only through you. You should understand God works through others as well as you, too. This way, we can accomplish everything beautifully in harmony.

Joseph acknowledged the work of God completely. So, when Jacob acted the opposite of what he had thought to be proper, he changed his opinion right away and followed his father's will. At first, he changed the position of his father's right hand and put it on

Manasseh the first son, asking him to bless Manasseh. But he didn't insist upon his opinion. He just expressed his opinion.

So, Jacob also expressed that he had his reasons by saying, "I know, my son, I know." Especially, seeing that he crossed his arms to bless his grandsons, we can see God was urging his heart very strongly.

Joseph understood his father meant to do what he had done and didn't speak about it any further. Jacob was Joseph's father after all, and Joseph respected him spiritually. He didn't insist on his opinions, and nor did he ignore physical order just because he was higher in the spiritual order. He just committed everything into God's hands. He was showing the form of 'true service'.

God is the Master of all the worlds including the spiritual and physical worlds, and He governs all things. When He created all the worlds, He made physical order as well as spiritual order. Therefore, the spiritual order can be perfected when the physical order is also maintained.

Of course, spiritual order comes first when there is a conflict between the two. But if you ignore the physical order just by considering the spiritual order, we cannot say it is to truly follow the spiritual order. God follows the spiritual order precisely without violating the physical order as well.

'True service' is accomplished when both spiritual and physical orders are maintained in harmony. Then, what do we have to do to have the harmony of spiritual order and physical order?

Even if you are higher in the spiritual order, you should honor the physical order. Conversely, even if you have older age, more experience, or higher position in physical order, you should understand that spiritual order comes first. The harmony of the spiritual and physical orders can be kept when everyone has this kind of attitude.

There is another reason why Joseph didn't insist on his opinion after he heard Jacob's words. It's because Joseph knew, for true blessings to come, the more important thing than receiving the blessing from the father was to actually make the blessings their own.

It's something Joseph realized through his own experiences. When God gave him such a great dream and a vision, he didn't just live a normal life believing God's promise would somehow be fulfilled. He did his best in every matter of his life, obeying the will of God to make his dream come true. Only then was God's promise fulfilled.

In the same way, even if Jacob gave greater blessing to Ephraim than to Manasseh, the actual blessing they received from God would be different depending on what kinds of actions they took. We can see the result of the blessing given by Jacob in the history of Israel.

Jacob was a man of God, and his blessings were effective. So, greater blessing was given to the descendants of Ephraim. The great leader, Joshua, was from the tribe of Ephraim. They received the central area when the land in Canaan was distributed among the twelve tribes. They had much greater influence than did Manasseh, too.

But later, they did evil things that were against God's will. When King Saul died and David was taking the throne, some of Saul's followers enthroned Ish-bosheth, Saul's son. Here, the tribe of Ephraim took their side. Furthermore, after Solomon's death, they stood against the tribe of Judah who had sovereignty and took a leading role in establishing the Northern Kingdom.

The first king of the Northern Kingdom, Jeroboam, was from the tribe of Ephraim. The Northern Kingdom of Israel that was established with Ephraim in its center began to worship idols and increasingly distanced itself from God. On the outside, they were influential and powerful, but they were corrupt inside.

What finally became of Ephraim? We can see that the name is excluded from the list of twelve tribes of Israel in Revelation chapter 7. The lesson here is that even if we have received prayer for great promises and blessings of God, it is up to us to actually bring down those blessings.

For the words of blessing to be fulfilled, there has to be the process in which we expend our effort to actually change ourselves. This is to be in accordance with justice. When God gives us promises of blessings, they are usually accompanied with some conditions.

Therefore, in order for God's words of blessings to come to complete fruition, we should not just hope for the outcome; we should be faithful in every step toward it as well. The words of blessing given by God will be realized as perfect fruit only when we understand God's will correctly at each moment and faithfully do all the things that we ought to do.

4. Jacob Gives More Inheritance to Joseph

Then Israel said to Joseph, "Behold, I am about to die, but God will be with you, and bring you back to the land of your fathers. I give you one portion more than your brothers, which I took from the hand of the Amorite with my sword and my bow." (48:21-22)

Jacob gave one portion more to Joseph than to other sons. Does that mean Jacob had favoritism until the end? No, it does not.

Joseph played the most important role in the process of forming the nation of Israel through the twelve tribes. He played such an important role in that process that we could even say everything was possible thanks to him alone.

Also, Joseph was loved and acknowledged by God the most among the twelve brothers, so it was only natural he received biggest blessing. For this reason God moved Jacob's heart to bless Joseph more than other brothers.

Now, how do you think Jacob's last will was fulfilled later? The sons of Israel came out of Egypt about 400 years later and went back to the land of their forefathers. They were only 70 in number when they went to Egypt, but after 400 years, they multiplied so much.

They had more than 600,000 young men who could fight in a war. If you include women, children, and older individuals, it would be well beyond 2 million.

The sons of Israel became a great nation of people now, and when they went to the land of Canaan, Joseph's two sons Ephraim and Manasseh were each considered as a tribe and received their own portion of land respectively. After all, Joseph received double of what other brothers received.

Those who are loved by God, they have good reasons to be loved by God. Therefore, we should not be jealous when others seem to be loved by God more than we are. It is important to understand the reason why they are loved and blessed by God more than others.

Psalm 119:2 says, *"How blessed are those who observe His testimonies, who seek Him with all their heart."* So much blessed are those who believe in God the Creator, keep His Word, and seek Him with all their heart, namely those who love God and earnestly seek Him.

Galatians 6:7 says, *"Do not be deceived, God is not mocked; for whatever a man sows, this he will also reap."* We cannot be loved or blessed by God while we are just doing what we ought to be doing to be seen and acknowledged. Joseph was loved and blessed greatly because he always kept God's Word, loved God with all his heart, and sought and longed for Him all the time.

Joseph

Chapter 11

Jacob's Death and Last Will

Jacob Summons His Sons before His Death

Reuben Loses His Birthright

Simeon and Levi Receive Retribution for their Wickedness

Prophecy of the Coming of the Messiah through Judah

Jacob's Last Will for Zebulun, Issachar, and Dan

Jacob's Last Will for Gad, Asher, and Naphtali

Jacob's Last Will for Joseph and Benjamin

Jacob's Request for His Burial in Canaan

1. Jacob Summons His Sons before His Death

Then Jacob summoned his sons and said, "Assemble yourselves that I may tell you what will befall you in the days to come. Gather together and hear, O sons of Jacob; and listen to Israel your father." (49:1-2)

Jacob was reunited with his son, Joseph, who he thought had been dead, and lived in Egypt for 17 years. He was thankful all those years. He prayed before God, "It's not that I had no regrets at all at each moment of my life, but now I thank You, God, that in Your precious intervention, You changed me and guided me, and now You let me beget these many children, and these children receive blessings of God."

Before his death, Jacob summoned his twelve sons and left his last will. He said, "I may tell you what will befall you in the days to come." These words were not coming from his personal opinions. God is the only One who knows the future.

Jacob's last will was given solely by the inspiration of God. His last words were fulfilled through his descendants in the future. Jacob's twelve sons who were to become the fathers of the twelve tribes received the prophecies, but it didn't mean the prophecies would indiscriminately befall everyone who belonged to each tribe.

It means each person would receive different blessings depending on their deeds. Even in the tribe that received words of blessing, there could be those who wouldn't receive blessings. Even in those tribes that received curses, there could be people who would receive blessings.

If we consider only the current state of the twelve sons at that moment, it seems befitting that the Messiah, Jesus, had to come through the tribe of Joseph. However, Jesus came through the tribe of Judah that had a shameful family history. It did not occur because Judah was particularly excellent or perfect.

God knew that, just before the Messiah would be born, a person called Joseph would be born and what kind of heart he would have. Moreover, God knew what kind of heart Mary had, who was going to be his wife. God also knew what kind of reaction Joseph would show when he came to know his fiancée Mary was pregnant before they came together (Matthew 1:19). God chose this man and that woman so that Jesus would be raised in a good family.

God sees the future as well as the things of the present, and He works in the most appropriate ways. Such was the case when He was giving His words to Jacob's sons. Yes, His words were given according to how they had been acting, but He also saw the goodness of their hearts and what kinds of minds they had.

Furthermore, depending on each individual's acts, they received different measures of blessings, even though they belonged to the same tribe. This is God's justice. God didn't form the nation of Israel only through the descendants of Joseph who had good heart. He formed the nation through all twelve sons of Jacob and worked according to the heart and deeds of each one of them.

2. Reuben Loses His Birthright

Reuben, you are my firstborn; my might and the beginning of my strength, preeminent in dignity and preeminent in power. Uncontrolled as water, you shall not have preeminence, because you went up to your father's bed; then you defiled it—he went up to my couch. (49:3-4)

Jacob started off with Reuben in giving his last will. In the history of Israel, especially during the era of the tribal leaders, the meaning that the firstborn carried was significant. Reuben was at a position where he could be guaranteed many kinds of things.

"Preeminent in dignity and preeminent in power" explains the authority given to the firstborn. Dignity is the respect and honor that cannot be overpowered. "Preeminent" is to be beyond measures and to transcend all kinds of powers. To be "preeminent in power" means Reuben was guaranteed the absolute authority as the firstborn.

However Reuben did not receive the blessing of the firstborn after all. It's because he made a great wall of sin that stopped his blessing. He committed adultery with Jacob's concubine Bilhah. When it happened, Jacob just covered his fault. He did so in order to save everyone. But it doesn't mean Reuben's sin disappeared. Even though Jacob just covered his fault, Reuben should have repented before God to demolish the wall of sin or he would have to face punishment in God's justice.

Even if he didn't receive the punishment on this earth, he would be judged even to the last penny. Nobody can escape the Great Judgment.

In the case of Reuben, at the time he committed a sin, Jacob didn't reveal it, but eventually his birthright was taken away later. He also received the prophecy that his tribe would not excel. It was the retribution for his sin. And in the actual history of Israel, there was no one who turned out to be a great judge, a prophet, or a king from the tribe of Reuben. Dathan and Abiram can be considered leaders during the life in wilderness after the Exodus, but they stood with Korah who had rebelled against Moses, and were destroyed.

Now, did God give His word to Reuben and his descendants intending it to mean something like "It's the destiny of your tribe, and you can't help it; you just have to accept it"? God wanted Reuben to repent. God wanted his descendants to keep this word in mind and to avoid going the wrong way.

If they would not repent and just perish anyway, and if the destiny of Reuben and his tribe could not be altered no matter how much they tried, God would have had no need to mention his previous fault in the first place. The reason why God reminded Reuben of his fault was that He wanted him to repent and receive salvation and blessings.

What if God keeps quiet about people's faults all the time? They wouldn't repent of their wrongdoings, thereby suffering from tests and trials and eventually reaching death. Therefore, God points out and reveals sins because He wants us to come to repentance and receive salvation as said in Ephesians 5:13, *"But all things become visible when they are exposed by the light, for everything that becomes visible is light."* It is so because of His love.

3. Simeon and Levi Receive Retribution for their Wickedness

Simeon and Levi are brothers; their swords are implements of violence. Let my soul not enter into their council; let not my glory be united with their assembly; because in their anger they slew men, and in their self-will they lamed oxen. Cursed be their anger, for it is fierce; and their wrath, for it is cruel. I will disperse them in Jacob, and scatter them in Israel. (49:5-7)

After he gave his last words to his first son, Jacob gave his last words to Simeon and Levi. He referred to them as "implements of violence" because of the things they had done to Shechem.

Jacob once stayed in front of the city of Shechem when he returned to Canaan after staying with his uncle Laban in Paddan-aram for 20 years. One of those days Jacob's daughter Dinah went into the city of Shechem to see the women there and was raped by Shechem, the chief of the city. Shechem later came to Jacob with his father Hamor asking for the permission to marry Dinah.

Jacob's sons said all men of the city of Shechem had to be circumcised for Shechem to marry their sister. The suggestion was accepted immediately. However, while the men of Shechem were suffering the pain of circumcision, Dinah's brothers who were born of the same mother attacked the city and killed all men there. They paid back evil with evil.

Of course, Shechem's sin was not trivial, but it doesn't mean Simeon's and Levi's retribution could be justified. If they had really revered God, they should have left everything to God rather than taking the matter into their own hands.

Because Simeon and Levi brutally killed many people with their cunning scheme, Jacob gave them words in retribution for their evil. He said, "Their swords are implements of violence. Let my soul not enter into their council; let not my glory be united with their assembly." He was saying to everyone in later generations that they must never partake in evil in any situation.

Psalm 1:1 says, *"How blessed is the man who does not walk in the counsel of the wicked, nor stand in the path of sinners, nor sit in the seat of scoffers!"* Therefore, in order to receive blessing from God, we must never agree with or take sides with those who are acting with evil schemes.

After they received the words saying, "I will disperse them in Jacob, and scatter them in Israel," what do you think happened to them later? The number of people in the tribe of Simeon kept on decreasing during the life in the wilderness after the Exodus. For this reason, when the land in Canaan was being allocated to the tribes, they did not receive their land independently as one tribe, but they only received it as a part of the tribe of Judah.

The tribe of Levi did not receive any land either; they were dispersed all over Israel. On the surface, these two tribes look similar, but the spiritual meaning was different. The tribe of Levi was scattered all over the country, but they had the holy duty to serve in the tabernacle, and their portion was supplied by all the other eleven tribes.

These two tribes received the same kind of prophecy from Jacob, but why were their respective destinies so different? It's because their deeds in later generations were very different.

In Exodus 32, we read that people made a golden calf and worshipped it while Moses went up to Mt. Sinai to receive the Commandments from God. God's wrath fell upon them. Moses said, *"Whoever is for the LORD, come to me!"* (v. 36) and immediately all the sons of Levi gathered together to him. They received words of blessing for this act.

In Numbers 25, while the sons of Israel remained in Shittim, they played harlot with Moabite women. They didn't just play harlot with them. They ate and bowed down together with the Moabite women who were worshipping idols. Finally, plague spread among the sons of Israel due to God's wrath and numerous people died.

In order to stop this wrath of God, Moses ordered the judges to kill those who had bowed down to Baal of Peor. Even in that situation there was a man in Israel who brought a Midianite woman into his tent. Unfortunately, he was from the tribe of Simeon. Now, a Levi called Phinehas went into that tent and killed both of them. The plague stopped immediately.

Now God gave the words of promise to the descendants of Phinehas through Moses: *"Phinehas the son of Eleazar, the son of Aaron the priest, has turned away My wrath from the sons of Israel in that he was jealous with My jealousy among them, so that I did not destroy the sons of Israel in My jealousy. Therefore say, 'Behold, I give him My covenant of peace; and it shall be for him and his descendants after him, a covenant of a perpetual priesthood, because he was jealous for his God and made atonement for the sons of Israel'"* (Numbers 25:11-13).

The tribe of Levi received the promises of blessing by being on God's side when the sons of Israel were committing grave sins. They were dispersed among the Israelites as Jacob prophesied, but they were chosen to do the blessed duty of serving God. As explained, rather than the word of God being blessing or curse, the kind of attitude we have when we receive it matters more. Even if we have received a curse, it can change into a blessing depending on what kinds of acts we show before God.

4. Prophecy of the Coming of the Messiah through Judah

Judah, your brothers shall praise you; your hand shall be on the neck of your enemies; your father's sons shall bow down to you. Judah is a lion's whelp; from the prey, my son, you have gone up. He couches, he lies down as a lion, and as a lion, who dares rouse him up? The scepter shall not depart from Judah, nor the ruler's staff from between his feet, until Shiloh comes, and to him shall be the obedience of the peoples. He ties his foal to the vine, and his donkey's colt to the choice vine; he washes his garments in wine, and his robes in the blood of grapes. His eyes are dull from wine, and his teeth white from milk. (49:8-12)

A word of blessing was given to the fourth son Judah. In the past, Judah played a vital role in saving Joseph's life when all the brothers were trying to kill him. Also, when Benjamin was in a situation to become a slave in Egypt, accused of being a thief, Judah stepped forward and volunteered to become a slave in Benjamin's place.

We can see that Judah understood his father's heart to some

extent and cared about him. We can also infer that he had the most love for his brothers second only to Joseph.

Jacob said to Judah, "Your brothers shall praise you." He prophesied Judah's descendants would be praised by other tribes and become the head among them. As prophesied, David came from the tribe of Judah and he became the king of the united kingdom of Israel and was praised by Israel as a whole. This was also the fulfillment of the prophecy, "Your father's sons shall bow down to you."

The prophecy of blessing, "Your hand shall be on the neck of your enemies" was also fulfilled when David and Solomon subdued all the neighboring countries that stood against Israel. However, the fundamental meaning of the above expression is that Jesus, who would come from the tribe of Judah, would demolish the camp of the enemy devil and Satan and complete His duty as the Savior.

Jacob continued to say, "Judah is a lion's whelp; from the prey, my son, you have gone up. He couches, he lies down as a lion, and as a lion, who dares rouse him up?" As prophesied, King David, from the tribe of Judah, expanded the territory and strengthened the country.

A scepter is a staff or baton borne by a sovereign as an emblem of authority. Therefore, "The scepter shall not depart from Judah, nor the ruler's staff from between his feet" means their sovereignty will continue. This prophecy is followed by another clue that Jesus would come from the tribe of Judah.

It says, "Until Shiloh comes" and Shiloh stands for Messiah.

Also, as said "and to him shall be the obedience of the peoples" all creation would kneel and bow down before the Lord, who is the King of kings and Lord of lords.

Judah received not only spiritual blessings but also abundant material blessings, too. It's because one receives the blessing of prosperity in all things as his soul prospers.

Jacob said, "He ties his foal to the vine, and his donkey's colt to the choice vine; he washes his garments in wine, and his robes in the blood of grapes. His eyes are dull from wine, and his teeth white from milk." It was a prophecy about peace, prosperity, and affluence that would be given in the land of Canaan flowing with milk and honey.

5. Jacob's Last Will for Zebulun, Issachar, and Dan

Zebulun will dwell at the seashore; and he shall be a haven for ships, and his flank shall be toward Sidon. Issachar is a strong donkey, lying down between the sheepfolds. When he saw that a resting place was good and that the land was pleasant, he bowed his shoulder to bear burdens, and became a slave at forced labor. Dan shall judge his people, as one of the tribes of Israel. Dan shall be a serpent in the way, a horned snake in the path, that bites the horse's heels, so that his rider falls backward. For Your salvation I wait, O LORD. (49:13-18)

Jacob prophesied that Zebulun would dwell at the seashore. As prophesied, the tribe of Zebulun received the land between the Mediterranean and the Sea of Galilee. According to the Jewish historian Josephus, Zebulun later expanded power to the coastal areas of the Mediterranean.

About Issachar, Jacob said, "Issachar is a strong donkey, lying down between the sheepfolds. When he saw that a resting place was good and that the land was pleasant, he bowed his shoulder to bear burdens, and became a slave at forced labor." As it was said "a strong donkey," Issachar became a big tribe. However, they did not become influential or prominent but were mostly engaged in farming or hard labor.

About Dan, Jacob said, "Dan shall judge his people, as one of the tribes of Israel. Dan shall be a serpent in the way, a horned snake in the path, that bites the horse's heels, so that his rider falls backward. For Your salvation I wait, O LORD."

The Bible mentions Dan as the name of a place. The original name of this place was Laish. The sons of Dan took that land and named it 'Dan'. The problem is that this place later became the base of idolatry.

The united kingdom of Israel was divided into two at the time of King Rehoboam the son of Solomon. Jeroboam the king of the northern kingdom of Israel was afraid that people might want to go down to the Jerusalem Temple in the southern kingdom of Judah. So, he made two golden calves and let the people worship them to prevent them from going to Jerusalem. One of them was located in Bethel and the other in Dan. Naturally Dan became the base of idolatry. The sons of Dan were quick to become imbued with idolatry (1 Kings 12:27-30).

Many people went the way of death worshiping idols. About this Dan, Jacob prophesied, "Dan shall be a serpent in the way, a horned snake in the path, that bites the horse's heels, so that his rider falls backward." Eventually, the name of Dan was excluded among the names of the twelve tribes of Israel in the book of Revelation.

It is also said, "Dan shall judge his people, as one of the tribes of Israel." However, it doesn't mean they would judge the people as the judge. It means the action of the tribe of Dan would serve as a standard of judgment. Namely, those who would act like the tribe of Dan would face destruction.

God still wanted the tribe of Dan to repent and receive salvation (1 Timothy 2:4). At the end of the Jacob's words toward Dan, he said, "For Your salvation I wait, O LORD." He was asking Dan to seek God's grace without losing hope. Jacob was asking God for His mercy and grace on behalf of his son Dan.

6. Jacob's Last Will for Gad, Asher, and Naphtali

As for Gad, raiders shall raid him, but he will raid at their heels. As for Asher, his food shall be rich, and he will yield royal dainties. Naphtali is a doe let loose, he gives beautiful words. (49:19-21).

Jacob prophesied about Gad, "As for Gad, raiders shall raid him, but he will raid at their heels." It means they were very brave. Moses also spoke about Gad's valor in Deuteronomy 33:20, *"Blessed is the one who enlarges Gad; he lies down as a lion, and tears the arm, also the crown of the head."*

When David was at Ziklag while he was running from King Saul, some warriors from the tribe of Gad were with him, and it is said about them, *"...mighty men of valor, men trained for war, who could handle shield and spear, and whose faces were like the faces of lions, and they were as swift as the gazelles on the mountains"* (1 Chronicles 12:8).

About Asher, it is said, "As for Asher, his food shall be rich, and he will yield royal dainties." After the conquering of the Canaan land, the tribe of Asher received the fertile, plain lands near the Mediterranean. They had abundant harvest of wheat and oil, which was then supplied to the royal palace.

The tribe of Asher was not particularly prominent, but they led a comfortable life thanks to their geographical advantage.

It is said about Naphtali, "Naphtali is a doe let loose, he gives beautiful words." This tribe had the image of agile warrior worthy to be compared to a doe let loose.

As a matter of fact, during the time of judges, Barak, from the tribe of Naphtali, helped the prophetess Deborah in saving Israel

(Judges 4:6, 5:15). They also played an important role when Gideon was attacking the Midianites (Judges 6:35, 7:23).

In Judges 5, we can read that Deborah and Barak, the son of Abinoam, sang on that day. As Jacob prophesied, we can see that they were excellent in singing, too.

7. Jacob's Last Will for Joseph and Benjamin

Joseph is a fruitful bough, a fruitful bough by a spring; its branches run over a wall. The archers bitterly attacked him, and shot at him and harassed him; but his bow remained firm, and his arms were agile, from the hands of the Mighty One of Jacob (From there is the Shepherd, the Stone of Israel), from the God of your father who helps you, and by the Almighty who blesses you with blessings of heaven above, blessings of the deep that lies beneath, blessings of the breasts and of the womb. The blessings of your father have surpassed the blessings of my ancestors up to the utmost bound of the everlasting hills; may they be on the head of Joseph, and on the crown of the head of the one distinguished among his brothers. Benjamin is a ravenous wolf; in the morning he devours the prey, and in the evening he divides the spoil. All these are the twelve tribes of Israel, and this is what their father said to them when he blessed them. He blessed every one of them with the blessing appropriate to each one. (49:22-28)

The eleventh son Joseph received great blessing from his father Jacob. Jacob said, "Joseph is a fruitful bough, a fruitful bough by a spring; its branches run over a wall."

Just as trees planted by the stream of water would not run dry even in drought, Joseph's descendants would prosper and enjoy abundance, thereby bringing their positive influence upon other tribes as well. Jacob continued to say that, even when there were enemies, Joseph would overwhelmingly defeat them by the help of God.

It is also said, "...blessings of heaven above, blessings of the deep that lies beneath, blessings of the breasts and of the womb." And this blessing is said to have surpassed the blessings of Jacob's ancestors, and it would be fulfilled completely without any change eternally. Jacob also prophesied Joseph's sons would excel the most among all tribes of Israel. As prophesied, Joseph's sons later received the central part of Canaan land as their inheritance and enjoyed abundant lives.

Joseph received the most abundant and most excellent blessing, which means that he actually received the birthright. He took the portion of two tribes through his sons Manasseh and Ephraim. They became the symbol of blessings that the people of later generation would say, *"May God make you like Ephraim and Manasseh!"* (Genesis 48:20)

Lastly, Jacob said to Benjamin, "Benjamin is a ravenous wolf; in the morning he devours the prey, and in the evening he divides the spoil."

This shows the aggression of the tribe of Benjamin. Benjamin was the son of Jacob's beloved wife Rachel, and he could have given Benjamin greater blessings. But all the words that came out of Jacob's mouth were inspired by God Himself.

As Jacob prophesied, the tribe of Benjamin had many famous archers and stone-throwers. They didn't form a very big tribe, but after the conquest of Canaan land, they took important cities such as Jericho, Bethel, Gibeon, Ramah, Mizpah, and Jerusalem.

Later, when Israel was divided into the northern and southern kingdoms, the tribe of Benjamin was the only tribe among Israel that united with Judah and served David and his family. The greatest apostle in the New Testament era, the apostle Paul was also from the house of Benjamin.

God knows everything and pays us back according to our deeds. Jacob did not just give blessings or curses at random and at his own discretion. They were all proclaimed by God's inspiration.

All those words were given precisely according to the past of the twelve sons and their future deeds. Also, different words were given depending on what kind of heart and mind each one of them had and how appropriate and worthy they were to be used as God's instruments.

After all, all those prophecies were fulfilled later. But as mentioned in the beginning, not every word of blessing or curse was applied indiscriminately to everyone in the same tribe. The general flow of words spoken of each tribe was fulfilled as prophesied, but different individuals received different blessings according to their deeds before God and according to whether or not they followed the will of God.

8. Jacob's Request for His Burial in Canaan

Then he charged them and said to them, "I am about to be gathered to my people; bury me with my fathers in the cave that is in the field of Ephron the Hittite, in the cave that is in the field of Machpelah, which is before Mamre, in the land of Canaan, which Abraham bought along with the field from Ephron the Hittite for a burial site. There they buried Abraham and his wife Sarah, there they buried Isaac and his wife Rebekah, and there I buried Leah — the field and the cave that is in it, purchased from the sons of Heth." When Jacob finished charging his sons, he drew his feet into the bed and breathed his last, and was gathered to his people. (49:29-33)

Just before his death, Jacob remembered his life and gave thanks from the depth of his heart to God who guided him and intervened in his life so delicately.

He cheated his father and brother and had to run away to his uncle's house. The trials for 20 years there were very difficult. However, he could feel that all those things came from God's love who wanted to change him and make him a perfect person.

He realized his methodologies and all his efforts were meaningless because they came out of his own wisdom and all was in vain and painful to him that he had done to go ahead of others and to fulfill what he had desired. He also realized that his 'self' and ego could be revealed by God's intervention, and he came to notice them and demolish them by God's grace.

He was thankful that he could now leave behind all the things that caused him sorrow, pain, or regret, and be at peace and rest in God's side. He deeply realized everything in this world was in vain like the morning fog.

After giving his last will to his sons who would become the head of the twelve tribes respectively, he asked them to bury him in the burial ground of his ancestors.

It was the cave that was in the field of Machpelah, which was before Mamre in the land of Canaan which Abraham had bought from Ephron the Hittite along with the field for a burial site. It was where they buried Abraham and his wife Sarah, Isaac and his wife Rebekah, and Jacob's wife Leah. He desired to be buried there because he faithfully believed in the word of God who had promised him He would lead him back to the Promised Land of Canaan.

Finally, after moving to Egypt and living there in the plan of God, Jacob, the father of Israel, breathed his last in peace in view of his children at the age of 147.

Add-in 5

Israel Became a Big People in Egypt

In Genesis 46, the number of Jacob's children who moved to and settled in Egypt was 70. With the help of Joseph who was the prime minister, they settled in the land of Goshen escaping the severe famine in Canaan. God led Jacob's children to multiply in Egypt that had a developed civilization and fertile land.

Egypt was in the central part of the ancient Near East. Jacob's children multiplied very quickly under the protection of Joseph who was the prime minister. After time passed, Joseph and everyone in his generation died, but the sons of Israel kept on increasing in number and became a big people (Exodus 1:7). This is the fulfillment of God's covenant that He had made with Abraham.

Genesis 15:4-5 says, *"Then behold, the word of the LORD came to him, saying, 'This man will not be your heir; but one who will come forth from your own body, he shall be your heir.' And He took him outside and said, 'Now look toward the heavens, and count the stars, if you are able to count them.' And He said to him, 'So shall your descendants be.'"*

In this plan of God the number of the sons of Israel increased exponentially, and when a new Pharaoh who didn't know about Joseph very well came in power, he wanted to keep them in check.

Exodus 1:9-10 says, *"He said to his people, 'Behold, the people of the sons of Israel are more and mightier than we. Come, let us deal wisely with them, or else they will multiply and in the event of war, they will also join themselves to those who hate us, and fight against us and depart from the land.'"*

Systematically they forced the sons of Israel into labor, and the king commanded the Hebrew midwives to kill all the newborn boys. Despite all these persecutions, God showed them grace and Israel only became greater and stronger (Exodus 1:11-21).

When Moses became the leader of the Exodus and led them out of Egypt, there were 600,000 young men who could fight in war (Exodus 12:37). If you include children, older people, and women, it would be well over two million people.

Chapter 12

Jacob's Funeral and Joseph's Death

Joseph Prepares Jacob's Funeral

"Let Me Go Up and Bury My Father"

Jacob's Grand Funeral Reveals God's Glory

"Do Not Be Afraid, For Am I in God's Place?"

"You Shall Carry My Bones Up from Here"

1. Joseph Prepares Jacob's Funeral

Then Joseph fell on his father's face, and wept over him and kissed him. Joseph commanded his servants the physicians to embalm his father. So the physicians embalmed Israel. Now forty days were required for it, for such is the period required for embalming. And the Egyptians wept for him seventy days. (50:1-3)

Joseph served his father Jacob for 17 years since Jacob had moved to Egypt. But Joseph couldn't serve him as much as he wished due to his weighty responsibilities. When his father died, Joseph couldn't help but shed tears of sadness. He kissed his father with all his love and affection.

Jacob is the father of Israel. God gave Jacob the new name 'Israel' when he came back from Paddan-aram and promised him that his descendants would prevail and take the Promised Land (Genesis 35:9-12). The people of 'Israel' was formed from his new name.

Jacob's twelve sons and Joseph's two sons were the foundation of the twelve tribes of Israel. This was the birth of the Israelites. With the death of Jacob, the era of tribal leaders centering Abraham, Isaac, and Jacob came to an end, and the history of 'Israel the Elect' began.

The funeral of Jacob, the father of Israel, was grand. Joseph commanded his servants who were the physicians to embalm his father. This alone took 40 days. This embalming meant that Jacob was mummified.

From the early days in Egypt they believed in resurrection, and for this reason they mummified the bodies of high officials. Of course, this resurrection is quite different from that of Christianity, but they did have longing for an eternal life and that is why they tried to keep the body for a long time.

Why did Joseph have an Egyptian funeral for his father? Joseph was already in deep spiritual level and he knew there was life after death and that the dead bodies would resurrect on the last day. For this reason he wanted to preserve the body as best as he could.

Jacob's funeral lasted for 70 days. Not only Jacob's family but Egyptians mourned his death for 70 days. It is said that they mourned for 72 days when the king died according to the funeral customs of that time, and thus, Jacob's funeral was an honor second only to the king.

It was not by force but voluntarily that Egyptians mourned for 70 days for the death of Jacob a foreigner. And the honor matching that of the king or royal family member couldn't have been bestowed upon a foreigner's funeral without the consent of Pharaoh and his servants. Such treatment was possible because they acknowledged the dedication and sacrifice of Joseph, and they loved and respected him to the utmost degree.

The Egyptians mourned Jacob's death out of their respect and love for their prime minister, Joseph. In brief, Joseph was a man of God, and thus his family also received great blessings through him.

2. "Let Me Go Up and Bury My Father"

When the days of mourning for him were past, Joseph spoke to the household of Pharaoh, saying, "If now I have found favor in your sight, please speak to Pharaoh, saying, 'My father made me swear, saying, "Behold, I am about to die; in my grave which I dug for myself in the land of Canaan, there you shall bury me." Now therefore, please let me go up and bury my father; then I will return.'" Pharaoh said, "Go up and bury your father, as he made you swear." (50:4-6)

There weren't many means of transportation at that time and it took a long time to travel to Canaan and come back. For Joseph to go to Canaan and come back, a temporary vacuum in government administration was inevitable. So Joseph would have had to get permission from Pharaoh to do so. Here, Joseph didn't ask Pharaoh himself, but let the household deliver his words to the Pharoah. It was because Joseph understood the heart of Pharaoh very well.

Pharaoh was completely dependent on Joseph for the administration of his kingdom. But because Joseph was not an

Egyptian, Pharaoh always had some lingering concern that Joseph might leave any time. In this situation, what if Joseph asked Pharaoh himself about leaving his post for some time? Pharaoh would have been quite worried.

For this reason Joseph sought men who could deliver his message to Pharaoh without making him worry. It was the people who were close to Pharaoh and had mutual trust. He delivered his message to the king through them so that the king would willingly give permission. It was delicate care and consideration for the one he was serving.

Joseph said to Pharaoh's household with an extremely humble attitude: "If now I have found favor in your sight, please speak to Pharaoh, saying, 'My father made me swear, saying, "Behold, I am about to die; in my grave which I dug for myself in the land of Canaan, there you shall bury me." Now therefore, please let me go up and bury my father; then I will return.'"

He was a savior of Egypt with high merit but he made no attempt to reveal it. Instead, he said he had found a great favor from the people there. He was always thankful that he was appointed as the prime minister and was entrusted with such a honorable duty even though he was a foreigner. Of course, this means he had friendship with them sharing many things, too. But Joseph always had the humble heart to lower himself and consider others better than himself rather than trying to show his good works.

Usually, if people have done anything well, they'd try to reveal it and earn the recognition and praise for it. Also, they think it is natural that if they did something for someone else, then that person should owe them something in return and repay the favor.

For this reason it is difficult for a person who wants something in return to be truly acknowledged and loved by people around him. Even though people receive help from such a person, they know that they'd have to return the favor someday so they can't be thankful from the depths of their hearts. Also, those who receive recognition and praise from others are already rewarded, so they don't have anything to receive from God who would reward them in secret (Matthew 6:2-4).

Joseph didn't want to reveal his work to anyone just because he had done such great things. But instead he humbled himself in his caring for and serving the people around him. For this reason people acknowledged and truly loved him. We can see the result of his service and humility though his father's funeral.

The household of Pharaoh asked Pharaoh to allow Joseph to keep his promise he had made to his father Jacob to bury him in the Canaan land. Pharaoh willingly gave him his permission.

3. Jacob's Grand Funeral Reveals God's Glory

So Joseph went up to bury his father, and with him went up all the servants of Pharaoh, the elders of his household and all the elders of the land of Egypt, and all the household of Joseph and his brothers and his father's household; they left only their little ones and their flocks and their herds in the land of Goshen. There also went up with him both chariots and horsemen; and it was a very great company. When they came to the threshing floor of Atad, which is beyond the Jordan, they lamented there with a very great and sorrowful lamentation; and he observed seven days mourning for his father. Now when the inhabitants of the land, the Canaanites, saw the mourning at the threshing floor of Atad, they said, "This is a grievous mourning for the Egyptians." Therefore it was named Abel-mizraim, which is beyond the Jordan. Thus his sons did for him as he had charged them; for his sons carried him to the land of Canaan and buried him in the cave of the field of Machpelah before Mamre, which Abraham had bought along with the field for a burial site from Ephron the Hittite. After he had buried his father, Joseph returned to Egypt, he and his brothers, and all who had gone up with him to bury his father. (50:7-14)

The funeral of Jacob, the father of Israel was accompanied by not only his family but also the servants of Pharaoh, elders, and the army as well. It was a nationwide funeral. It tells us what kind of attitude the king and the people of Egypt had for Jacob's funeral.

All this was the grace of God given to Jacob who had fulfilled his duty in God's providence. Also, it was possible because his son, Joseph, was respected and loved by Pharaoh and the people of Egypt.

It was also Joseph's intention to have a funeral as grand as possible; he wanted to reveal the glory of God. In the eyes of Egyptians, Jacob was just a foreigner and merely a tribal chief from a foreign place. Joseph wanted to let the people know that he was a man of God by having a big funeral. Joseph wanted to give glory to

God by showing what kinds of blessings and glory are given to those who are loved by God.

Usually, when people are in difficult situations, the merits and good work they have stored will be revealed. The substantial help they can receive from others becomes different depending on what kinds of relationships they had with others and how much they earned the heart of others. If you have been serving others and maintained good relationships with them, there will be many who will step up to help you.

Of course, we should help and care for not just those with whom we have good relationships but also those not. This is true love and goodness (Matthew 5:46-47). As God's children you shouldn't be nice only to those who are nice to you, nor should you show love desiring something in return. Whoever you are dealing with, you should seek their benefit, give to them first, and serve them willingly.

Joseph showed true love to serve the interests of others first while being the prime minister, and so his fruits were abundant. Namely, he could have his father's funeral with the honor of a royal family member, which was truly magnificent and grand.

The funeral procession that was accompanied by chariots and horsemen finally reached Canaan. After crossing the Jordan River, they mourned again for seven days at Atad. The sound of mourning was so loud that the Canaanites called that place Abel-mizraim, which means "This is a grievous mourning for the Egyptians." Then, Jacob's sons buried their father according to his last will in the cave of the field of Machpelah before Mamre, where Isaac and Abraham were also buried.

After all the funeral proceedings were over, Joseph returned immediately to Egypt. He carried out his promise to Pharaoh without delay. Joseph didn't think like, "I've just finished this big event and I need some rest. I've come to my homeland after decades, and I'd like to spend some time here." He was trusted by Pharaoh and the people around him because he was a man of his word.

It is very important to keep what we say. If we change our words or break our promises due to personal reasons thinking, "I have this new situation and they will understand," or "This much change is OK," then what will happen? We will lose our trust not only from God but also from other people.

4. "Do Not Be Afraid, For Am I in God's Place?"

When Joseph's brothers saw that their father was dead, they said, "What if Joseph bears a grudge against us and pays us back in full for all the wrong which we did to him!" So they sent a message to Joseph, saying, "Your father charged before he died, saying, 'Thus you shall say to Joseph, "Please forgive, I beg you, the transgression of your brothers and their sin, for they did you wrong."' And now, please forgive the transgression of the servants of the God of your father." And Joseph wept when they spoke to him. Then his brothers also came and fell down before him and said, "Behold, we are your servants." But Joseph said to them,

"Do not be afraid, for am I in God's place? As for you, you meant evil against me, but God meant it for good in order to bring about this present result, to preserve many people alive. So therefore, do not be afraid; I will provide for you and your little ones." So he comforted them and spoke kindly to them. (50:15-21)

After they came back to Egypt from the funeral, Joseph's brothers had a concern. Now that their father had died, they thought Joseph might want to take revenge for their past wrongdoing.

So, they asked Joseph to forgive them of their wrong toward him saying it was their father's wish. They couldn't even ask for forgiveness themselves, so they sent a messenger to deliver the message.

Joseph wept hearing their request. He had forgiven his brothers a long time ago, and he held no grudges at all. Instead, he served his brothers with all his best for the 17 years of their stay in Egypt. He was sad because his brothers didn't understand him at all.

But as a matter of fact, his brothers couldn't understand Joseph's heart. It's because they would not have been able to forgive Joseph if they had been in his shoes. They thought Joseph treated them nicely just because of their father. Now that their father had died, they couldn't help but worry.

Men of flesh look at others within their own frameworks of thinking. They make judgments about other people's hearts based on their own standards. And Joseph's heart was broken seeing this in his brothers. He had more sorrow when he thought,

"How can they have such concerns? How tormented they must be now!" A man of spirit like Joseph would feel sad when others don't understand him, but he is even more sorrowful because he understands the standpoint of others who are suffering due to their misunderstandings about him.

Joseph's brothers were not comfortable just by delivering the words of their father to Joseph, so they came before Joseph, fell down before him and asked for forgiveness. His brothers were saying to him, "We are your servants," yet Joseph didn't resent them and didn't say, "How come you don't understand my heart at all?" But rather, he comforted them saying, "Do not be afraid, for am I in God's place? As for you, you meant evil against me, but God meant it for good in order to bring about this present result, to preserve many people alive."

Joseph explained once again that his brothers did a very evil thing, but God caused all things to work for good and the whole family was saved through the incident. Furthermore, he said, "I will provide for you and your little ones." He put their minds at ease by promising them to provide for them and their children. This proves that Joseph reached a level of complete goodness in which he moved the heart of those who harmed him, and not only that, he could also give his life for them.

5. "You Shall Carry My Bones Up from Here"

Now Joseph stayed in Egypt, he and his father's household, and Joseph lived one hundred and ten years. Joseph saw the third generation of Ephraim's sons; also the sons of Machir, the son of Manasseh, were born on Joseph's knees. Joseph said to his brothers, "I am about to die, but God will surely take care of you and bring you up from this land to the land which He promised on oath to Abraham, to Isaac and to Jacob." Then Joseph made the sons of Israel swear, saying, "God will surely take care of you, and you shall carry my bones up from here." So Joseph died at the age of one hundred and ten years; and he was embalmed and placed in a coffin in Egypt. (50:22-26)

Joseph understood the great plan of God to form the nation of Israel in Egypt. He was sold as a slave into Egypt at the age of 17 and became the prime minister at the age of 30, and his family was moved to Egypt and laid the foundation for the formation of the nation of Israel, and he knew all this was in the great plan of God. For this reason he took care of his brothers and their children as best as he was able, even after Jacob's death.

Now Joseph was 110 years old. It was 93 years after he was sold as a slave into Egypt and 80 years after he interpreted Pharaoh's dream and became the prime minister. It had already been 50 years since he buried his father in the family burial ground. He had seen the third generation of Ephraim's children, and Manasseh's grandsons were also raised under Joseph's care.

Joseph maintained peace with Pharaoh, his servants, the people, those who were serving him, his father and his brothers. It was possible because he first had peace with God and then with himself. He followed the will of God with a good heart free of evil. He accepted and understood everybody and served them. He had no trouble with anybody.

He resolved all problems with the wisdom of goodness. And thus, there was nobody who was jealous of him or opposed him with hard-feelings. If you have peace with God and with yourself, you will have peace with others around you, thereby having peace of mind. The most important thing is the peace with God. You must never break peace with God in order to have peace with men.

Joseph never committed a sin even though he was wrongfully accused. Even when he was in jail, he didn't complain saying, "Why should I have suffered though I have lived only by God's will?" He only gave thanks and rejoiced. This is to pursue peace with God. When we pursue peace with God, it sometimes seems that peace with others might be broken, but actually great blessings will follow, and the peace with others will soon be restored, too.

Because he believed the love and faithfulness of God, he committed all situations into God's hands and considered everything in view of goodness. So, there was no reason for him to complain about anything; neither did he have ill-feelings or hatred against anybody.

In Exodus chapter 1, we can see how deeply Joseph was remembered by the Egyptians. A new king in Egypt who didn't know about Joseph came to power, and it was from this time that the persecution against the sons of Israel began. It was more than

300 years after Israel settled down in Egypt. What does it imply that the persecution against the sons of Israel began from this time?

It means the name and the merit of Joseph saving Egypt from seven years of famine was remembered in Egypt for hundreds of years, and a comfortable life was guaranteed for the sons of Israel during those years. They settled in Egypt and multiplied for a long time under the influence of Joseph, thereby forming a great people.

At his deathbed, Joseph said to his brothers, "I am about to die, but God will surely take care of you and bring you up from this land to the land which He promised on oath to Abraham, to Isaac and to Jacob." He believed that Israel wouldn't live in Egypt forever but they would form a big people and go back to the Canaan land.

For this reason Joseph made his children swear they'd take his bones when they'd move to Canaan later. He said, "God will surely take care of you, and you shall carry my bones up from here." He earnestly wanted to be buried in the Promised Land of God.

Joseph knew the sons of Israel would go back to the Promised Land of Canaan, yet he also knew that it wasn't going to be anytime soon. That is why he asked his children to take his bones when the Israelites would go to Canaan later. By making them swear they'd do so, Joseph also wished they'd never forget the fact that they'd have to go back to Canaan someday. He hoped that they'd not forget they'd have to go back to their original homeland, the Promised Land of God, even though their life in Egypt was good.

After fulfilling all the duties given by God, Joseph faced his death in peace in the view of his brothers. His last will was carried out hundreds of years later.

Exodus 13:19 says, *"Moses took the bones of Joseph with him, for he had made the sons of Israel solemnly swear, saying, 'God will surely take care of you, and you shall carry my bones from here with you.'"*

Also, Joshua 24:32 says, *"Now they buried the bones of Joseph, which the sons of Israel brought up from Egypt, at Shechem, in the piece of ground which Jacob had bought from the sons of Hamor the father of Shechem for one hundred pieces of money; and they became the inheritance of Joseph's sons."* Joseph's bones were buried in Shechem, after the allocation of lands among the sons of Israel.

My beloved God,
I give thanks to You, my God,
For even in the indiscretions of my youth
You considered me and guided me,
You led me into the truth.

Everything in my life has been peaceful
And all things have been prosperous.
It's been by the grace of the Father.
You considered a lowly person like me
And led me to be perfected.
You brought many people to kneel
Before the name of the LORD God.
You let me fulfill the providence of God.

My God, I give You thanks.

I close my eyes now,
However, in all things that remain,
Let God's will and providence be done.
Let the beam of grace always shine on everyone
So that they will not forget the grace of God.
Give many people more understanding in their hearts
That they should never forget God's grace,
And lead them in all their ways.

Joseph laid the foundation of the nation of Israel, the Elect, and saved so many lives. He rejoiced and gave thanks to God and believed in His good will in all kinds of trials. He always looked back on himself rather than putting the blame on others. He was just faithful in all aspects and completed all his duties.

And God made him prosper anywhere he went and let him be honored and loved by the people around him. All his hard-work and God's grace on him made him a great man of God who saved lives of many peoples.

Add-in 6

Funerals of Egyptians and Hebrews

A funeral is a ceremony or group of ceremonies held in connection with the burial or cremation of a dead person. The funerals of ancient Egyptians and Hebrews show clear distinction about their views of afterlife.

Egyptian Funerals

The religion and cultures of Egyptians showed their longing for life after death. They made mummies because they had a belief in resurrection. But they didn't think everyone could have a life after death. It was considered a privilege that could be enjoyed only by the Pharaohs, but as time passed they gradually began to believe everyone could have a life after death. In this regard, mummification, which was initially only for Pharaohs was later expanded to include high officials and eventually, ordinary people.

They removed the organs except for the heart, and the body was further dehydrated by placing it in natron, a naturally occurring salt, for seventy days. They wrapped the body about 20 times with linen bandages. The bandages were covered with a gum that modern research has shown is both a waterproofing agent and an antimicrobial agent.

Usually mummified bodies were kept in caves or pyramids, and these places were not just considered as graves but a space where the dead were living. They put some furniture and utensils for the deceased so that they wouldn't have inconvenience in their afterlife.

On the walls of the graves were paintings or writings of the deceased eating at a table, activities of their daily lives, or other religious activities. There were also small sculptures called Shabti. These sculptures were servants who would do the labor for the dead in the afterlife.

Hebrew Funerals

When people died, the Hebrews closed their eyes and washed the body (Acts 9:37). They then put frankincense or myrrh on the body and wrapped it with fine linen (Matthew 27:59; John 19:39-40). Then they moved the body to the burial ground. The relatives and friends followed this procession.

Generally the funeral lasted only a day and was held on the day of death. They tried to finish within the day because the high temperature caused the bodies to decay at a fast rate. However, a more important reason was to avoid being 'unclean' (Deuteronomy 21:23; John 19:31). Namely, it was considered unclean to touch a dead body (Numbers 5:2).

For graves they dug a hole mostly in caves or on hillsides. After the burial, they usually had a mourning period of 7 days (Genesis 50:10; 1 Samuel 31:13). It was an exception when they mourned for 70 days for Jacob and 30 days for Moses and Aaron (Numbers 20:29; Deuteronomy 34:8). Sometimes they made songs of lamentation to remember the deceased during the mourning period. One of the examples is the lamentation that David sang when Saul and Jonathan died (2 Samuel 1:19-27).

Also, in the mind of the Hebrews, not being buried after death was considered the greatest shame. For example, Jezebel was eaten by dogs and not buried (2 Kings 9:10), and it was such a shameful curse that couldn't be compared with anything else. Such were the cases with Jeroboam and Baasha. Jeroboam led the Northern Kingdom of Israel to worship idols (1 Kings 14:11), and Baasha followed Jeroboam's ways (1 Kings 16:4).

Hebrews didn't bury their dead along with material things. It was different from the Egyptians. They believed that men's souls went up above (Ecclesiastes 3:21), and the body that became dust would resurrect and reunite with the soul again (Daniel 12:2).

· Epilogue 1 ·

Joseph, the Passageway of God's Covenant

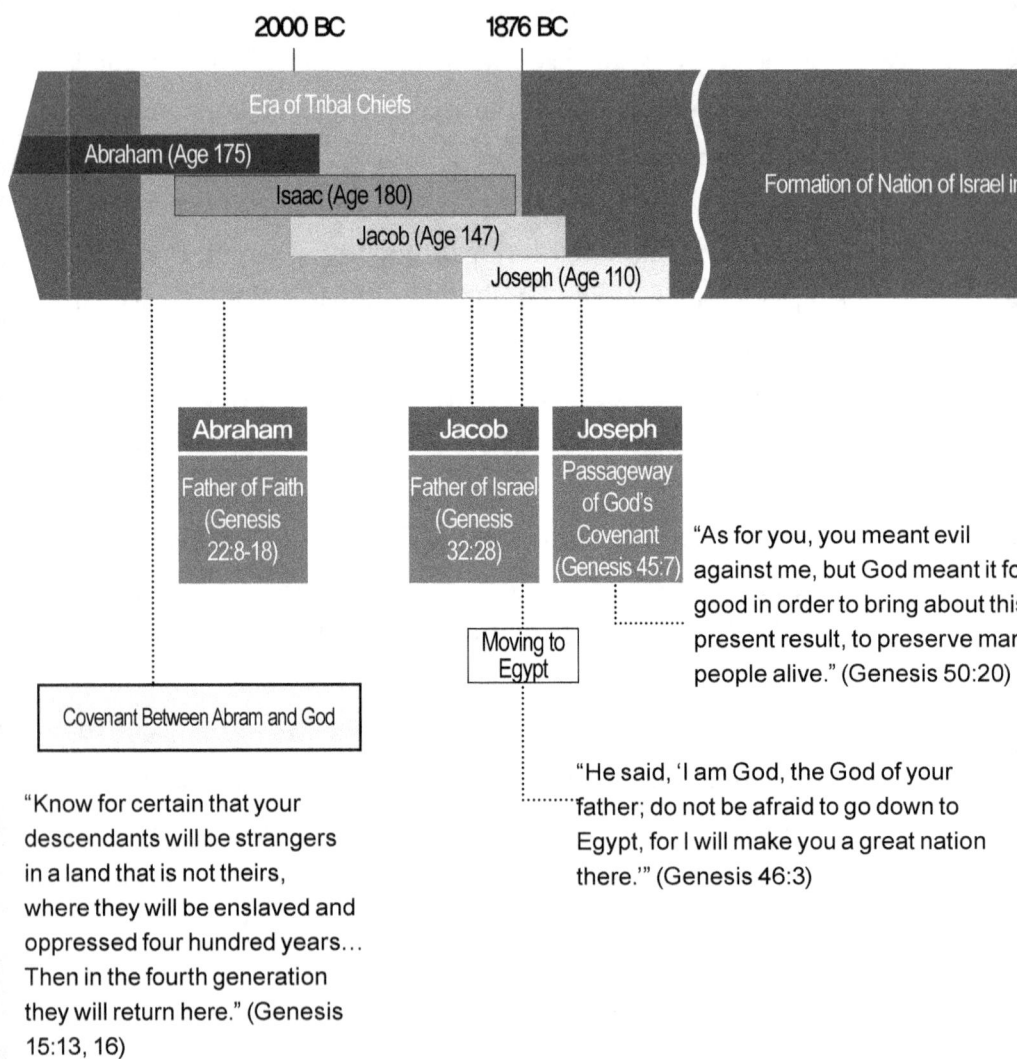

2000 BC — 1876 BC

Era of Tribal Chiefs

Abraham (Age 175)
Isaac (Age 180)
Jacob (Age 147)
Joseph (Age 110)

Formation of Nation of Israel in

Abraham
Father of Faith
(Genesis 22:8-18)

Jacob
Father of Israel
(Genesis 32:28)

Joseph
Passageway of God's Covenant
(Genesis 45:7)

"As for you, you meant evil against me, but God meant it for good in order to bring about this present result, to preserve many people alive." (Genesis 50:20)

Moving to Egypt

Covenant Between Abram and God

"Know for certain that your descendants will be strangers in a land that is not theirs, where they will be enslaved and oppressed four hundred years… Then in the fourth generation they will return here." (Genesis 15:13, 16)

"He said, 'I am God, the God of your father; do not be afraid to go down to Egypt, for I will make you a great nation there.'" (Genesis 46:3)

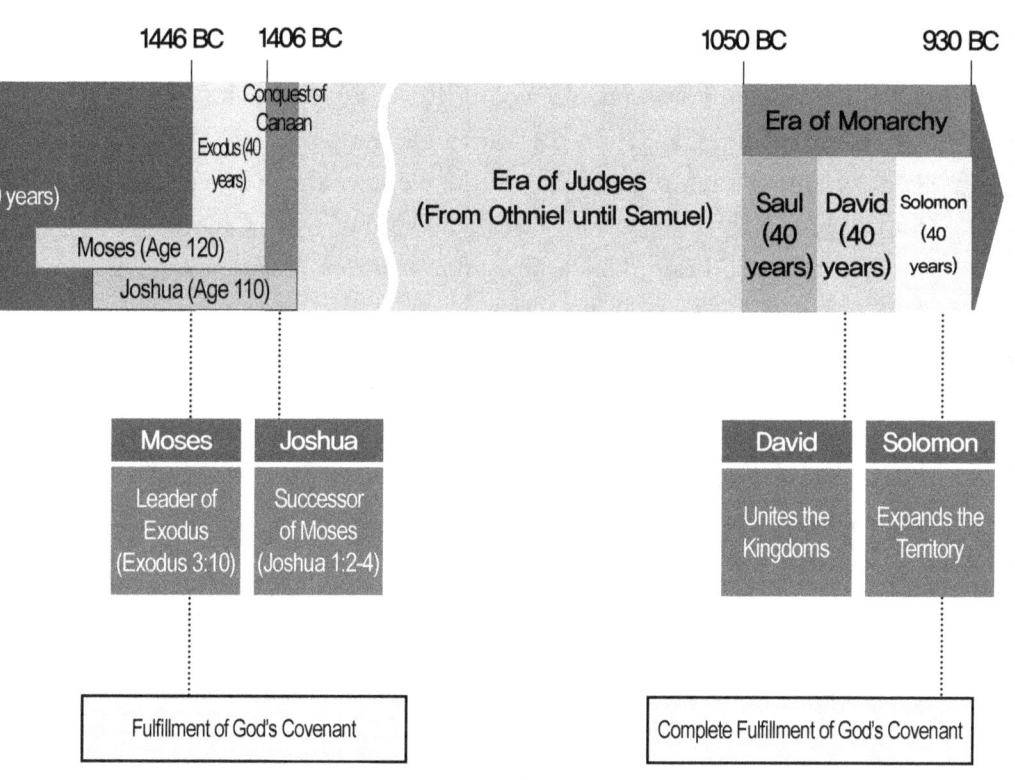

"Now it came about in the four hundred and eightieth year after the sons of Israel came out of the land of Egypt, in the fourth year of Solomon's reign over Israel, in the month of Ziv which is the second month, that he began to build the house of the LORD." (1 Kings 6:1)

"And at the end of four hundred and thirty years, to the very day, all the hosts of the LORD went out from the land of Egypt." (Exodus 12:41)

"So Joshua took the whole land, according to all that the LORD had spoken to Moses, and Joshua gave it for an inheritance to Israel according to their divisions by their tribes. Thus the land had rest from war." (Joshua 11:23)

"Now after this it came about that David defeated the Philistines and subdued them...

...the Moabites became servants to David, bringing tribute.

...And the LORD helped David wherever he went." (1 Chronicles 18:1, 2, 6)

"He was the ruler over all the kings from the Euphrates River even to the land of the Philistines, and as far as the border of Egypt." (2 Chronicles 9:26)

· Epilogue 2 ·

Flaming Torch Covenant and Fulfillment of the Prophecy

In Genesis 15, God showed Abram things to come in his dream. God said Abram's descendants would live in Egypt for 400 years and come back to Canaan in the fourth generation. After this was said, a flaming torch passed between the pieces of the sacrifice, and for this reason this covenant is also called Flaming Torch Covenant.

God said to Abram, *"Know for certain that your descendants will be strangers in a land that is not theirs, where they will be enslaved and oppressed four hundred years. But I will also judge the nation whom they will serve, and afterward they will come out with many possessions. As for you, you shall go to your fathers in peace; you will be buried at a good old age. Then in the fourth generation they will return here, for the iniquity of the Amorite is not yet complete"* (Genesis 15:13-16).

God said the sons of Israel would go to Egypt, and be enslaved and oppressed there 400 years. Namely, it was said Abraham's descendants would come back to Canaan after 400 years.

Acts 7:6 also mentions the 400 years saying, *"...they would be enslaved and mistreated for four hundred years."* But Exodus 12:40-41 says, *"Now the time that the sons of Israel lived in Egypt was four hundred and thirty years. And at the end of four hundred and thirty years, to the very day, all the hosts of the LORD went out from the land of Egypt."* It is said the duration is 430 years.

Galatians 3:17 also mentions 430 years saying, *"What I am saying is this: the Law, which came four hundred and thirty years later, does not invalidate a covenant previously ratified by God, so as to nullify the promise."*

So, where do these differences come from? Saying it was 400 years is based on the average lifespan of the people at the time. 100 years is considered one generation, and thus four generations was 400 years. Namely, 400 years is an approximation coming from the four generations. But the actual duration of time Israel stayed in Egypt was 430 years.

There are several explanations about the beginning point and end point of this 430 years, but generally if you consider Jacob and his family moved to Egypt in 1876 BC and the actual Exodus 1446 BC, it comes to 430 years.

300 years after Jacob's household settled in Egypt, they multiplied greatly and their population had become quite large. An Egyptian king who didn't know about Joseph felt threatened by the sons of Israel and tried to keep them in check. He enslaved them and forced them into hard labor. The sons of Israel cried out to God in suffering, and God heard them. He remembered the covenant He had made with Abraham and Isaac and Jacob.

Now, the fulfillment of God's promise that these people would come back to the land of their fathers in four generations was imminent. At the same time, the sins of people in Canaan were so prevalent that the punishment couldn't be postponed any longer. For this situation, God had prepared a man to lead the sons of Israel to the Canaan land. It was Moses.

"Then the king of Egypt spoke to the Hebrew midwives, one of whom was named Shiphrah and the other was named Puah; and he said, 'When you are helping the Hebrew women to give birth and see them upon the birthstool, if it is a son, then you shall put him to death; but if it is a daughter, then she shall live.' But the midwives feared God, and did not do as the king of Egypt had commanded them, but let the boys live." (Exodus 1:15-17)

"The daughter of Pharaoh came down to bathe at the Nile, with her maidens walking alongside the Nile; and she saw the basket among the reeds and sent her maid, and she brought it to her. When she opened it, she saw the child, and behold, the boy was crying. And she had pity on him and said, 'This is one of the Hebrews' children.'" (Exodus 2:5-6)

"'Take this child away and nurse him for me and I will give you your wages.' So the woman took the child and nursed him. The child grew, and she brought him to Pharaoh's daughter and he became her son. And she named him Moses, and said, 'Because I drew him out of the water.'" (Exodus 2:9-10)

Moses was raised as a prince of Egypt in God's plan, but he became a fugitive overnight because he killed an Egyptian who was physically abusing his people, a Hebrew man. He fled to Midian and tended the flock for 40 years. This was also God's plan to refine him and make him the leader of the Exodus.

When the time came, God set him up as the leader of his people and had him go to Pharaoh and demand him to let His people go. From Exodus chapter 5 onward, Pharaoh didn't comply and God inflicted Egypt with the ten plagues. Finally, the sons of Israel came out of Egypt under the leadership of Moses.

"Now the sons of Israel journeyed from Rameses to Succoth, about six hundred thousand men on foot, aside from children. A mixed multitude also went up with them, along with flocks and herds, a very large number of livestock." (Exodus 12:37-38)

"Now the time that the sons of Israel lived in Egypt was four hundred and thirty years. And at the end of four hundred and thirty years, to the very day, all the hosts of the LORD went out from the land of Egypt. It is a night to be observed for the LORD for having brought them out from the land of Egypt; this night is for the LORD, to be observed by all the sons of Israel throughout their generations." (Exodus 12:40-42)

God set the sons of Israel free as He had promised Abraham in the flaming torch covenant. Furthermore, He sent them out to the Promised Land with much wealth. We can see that all the events were in the providence of God including: Joseph being sold into Egypt as a slave, later becoming the prime minister there, his brothers moving to Egypt, and coming out of Egypt after 430 years.

The flaming torch covenant in Genesis 15 is one of the most essential covenants in the Bible. In historical sense, it is about the formation of Israel through the conquest of Canaan. But ultimately, it contains another important meaning: mankind that has been severed from God due to sins recovering the lost image of God and being born again as God's children.

· Epilogue 3 ·

Promise about the Canaan Land and Fulfillment

Making the flaming torch covenant with Abraham, God let him know the borders of the Canaan land that He would give to Abraham's descendants.

"On that day the LORD made a covenant with Abram, saying, 'To your descendants I have given this land, from the river of Egypt as far as the great river, the river Euphrates: the Kenite and the Kenizzite and the Kadmonite and the Hittite and the Perizzite and the Rephaim and the Amorite and the Canaanite and the Girgashite and the Jebusite.'" (Genesis 15:18-21)

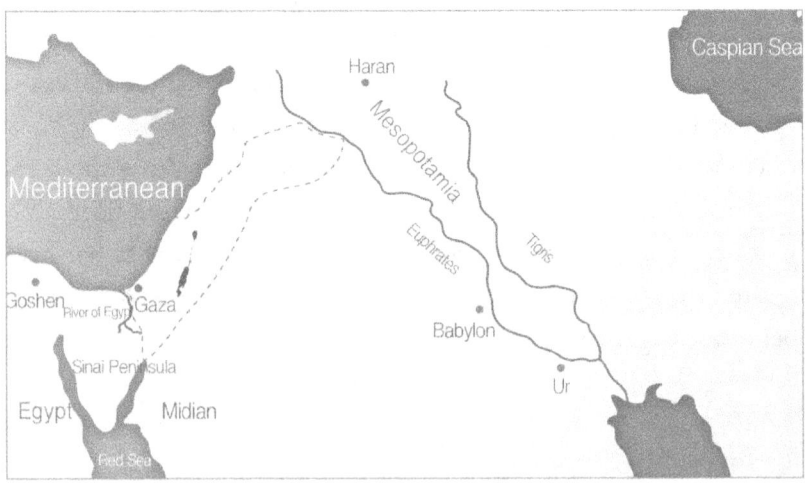

The Borders God Promised to Abraham

The southern border of Israel was the river of Egypt that passed southern part of Gaza and went into the Mediterranean (Joshua 15:4; 1 Kings 8:65), and the northern border was the Euphrates, which was the cradle for the Mesopotamian civilization (Deuteronomy 1:7, 11:24; Joshua 1:4).

After God told Abraham the area and borders of the land in detail, He spoke to him about the ten peoples in the land of Canaan. This means a conquest was required to take the land and they could have it if they trusted the covenant of God. This Promised Land was a beautiful land that was flowing with milk and honey.

"On the day when I chose Israel and swore to the descendants of the house of Jacob and made Myself known to them in the land of Egypt, when I swore to them, saying, I am the LORD your God, on that day I swore to them, to bring them out from the land of Egypt into a land that I had selected for them, flowing with milk and honey, which is the glory of all lands." (Ezekiel 20:5-6)

Exodus through Moses and Conquest of Canaan through Joshua

Just before the sons of Israel went into the Canaan land that was flowing with milk and honey, they camped at Moab, and God once again let Moses know the borders of all the lands north, south, east, and west.

"Your southern sector shall extend from the wilderness of Zin along the side of Edom, and your southern border shall extend from the end of the

Salt Sea eastward. Then your border shall turn direction from the south to the ascent of Akrabbim and continue to Zin, and its termination shall be to the south of Kadesh-barnea; and it shall reach Hazaraddar and continue to Azmon." (Numbers 34:3-4)

"As for the western border, you shall have the Great Sea, that is, its coastline; this shall be your west border. And this shall be your north border: you shall draw your border line from the Great Sea to Mount Hor." (Numbers 34:6-7)

"For your eastern border you shall also draw a line from Hazar-enan to Shepham," (Numbers 34:10)

"And the border shall go down to the Jordan and its termination shall be at the Salt Sea. This shall be your land according to its borders all around." (Numbers 34:12)

God told Moses the borders once again in order to give the people of Israel assurance and courage before the actual conquest. It was also to let it be known that Israel was established as God's Elect (Deuteronomy 26:19, 32:8).

However, in the actual conquest of the Canaan land, the sons of Israel couldn't take all the lands from Egypt to Euphrates, but they took most of what was promised by God.

The lands were allocated to each tribe by casting lots (Map 1), and you can see that it is in agreement with Jacob's prophecy as recorded in Genesis 49:1-28 for the most part. Especially, as Jacob blessed them, Ephraim and Manasseh received the fertile land in the

central part of Canaan.

David's United Kingdom and Expansion of Territory

After the death of Saul the first king of Israel, David was crowned by the tribe of Judah (2 Samuel 2:4). Seven years later David took the northern tribes who had crowned Ish-bosheth, the son of Saul. Now all tribes of Israel were united as one kingdom (2 Samuel 5:1-5).

As the kingdom was stabilized, David began to conquer the neighboring countries (2 Samuel 8:1-18). The territory was extended to Syria and Euphrates, and Israel became a very strong nation that acquired a great amount of spoils of war and received tributes from other countries.

"Now after this it came about that David defeated the Philistines and subdued them and took Gath and its towns from the hand of the Philistines. He defeated Moab, and the Moabites became servants to David, bringing tribute. David also defeated Hadadezer king of Zobah as far as Hamath, as he went to establish his rule to the Euphrates River." (1 Chronicles 18:1-3)

"Then David put garrisons among the Arameans of Damascus; and the Arameans became servants to David, bringing tribute. And the LORD helped David wherever he went." (1 Chronicles 18:6)

The expanded territory of Israel was three times bigger than the land they had at the time of the conquest of Canaan (Map 2). It was

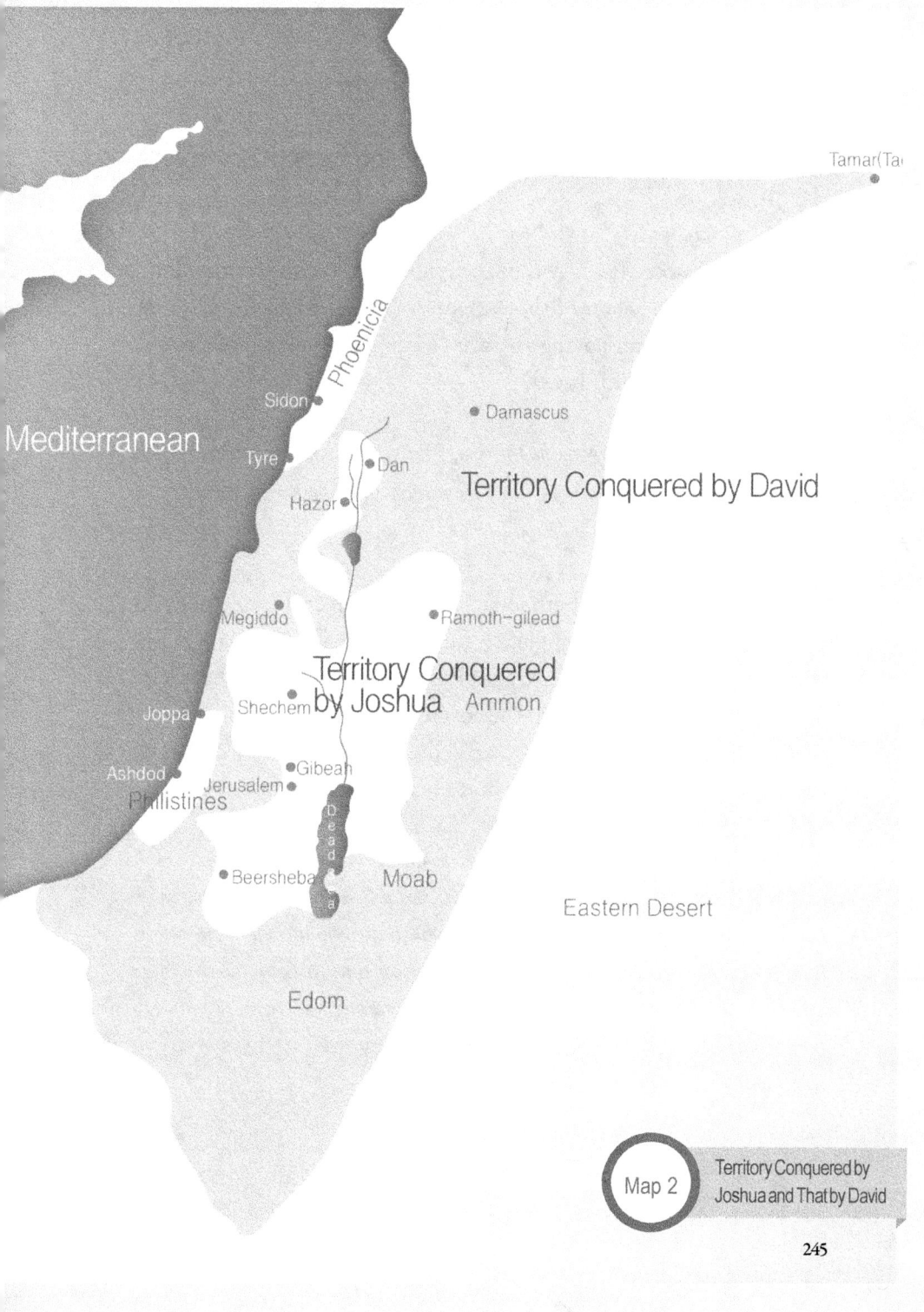

the fulfillment of God's covenant with Abraham.

God's Covenant Completely Fulfilled during Solomon's Reign

Solomon succeeded David in the reign over the united kingdom, and based on the power of this kingdom, he had control over a vast area of lands without having any war (Map 3). It was the fulfillment of God's covenant with Israel.

"He was the ruler over all the kings from the Euphrates River even to the land of the Philistines, and as far as the border of Egypt." (2 Chronicles 9:26)

God promised Abraham that He would give him all the land of Canaan, and it was completely fulfilled during Solomon's reign, which was around 970 BC to 930 BC (1 Kings 4:25; 2 Chronicles 9:26). It was 1,100 years after the covenant was made. The covenant of Abraham in Genesis 17 was fulfilled in the history of Israel, thereby confirming God is alive and He fulfills all His promises.

"I will make you exceedingly fruitful, and I will make nations of you, and kings will come forth from you. I will establish My covenant between Me and you and your descendants after you throughout their generations for an everlasting covenant, to be God to you and to your descendants after you. I will give to you and to your descendants after you, the land of your sojournings, all the land of Canaan, for an everlasting possession; and I will be their God." (Genesis 17:6-8)

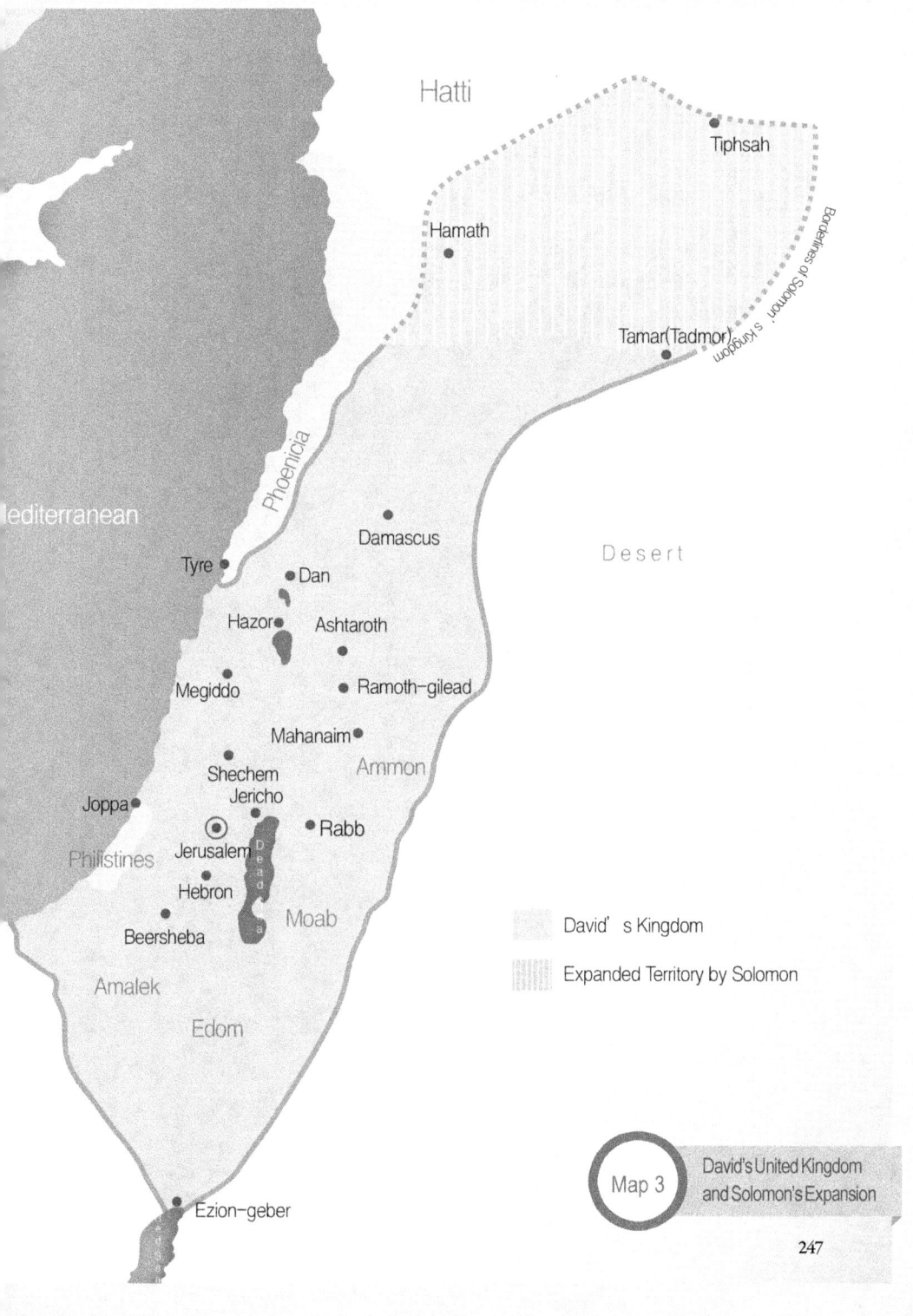

www.ingramcontent.com/pod-product-compliance
Lightning Source LLC
LaVergne TN
LVHW021808060526
838201LV00058B/3292